COVID GATE 2022

–

AGENDA 21 UNCOVERED

The Deep State Elite & Big Pharma Exposed!

Vaccines – The Great Reset – Global Crisis

2030-2050

Truth Leaks Books

GW00708176

Disclaimer

Staging the pandemic

What the world experiences at present is the probably biggest lie of the human history so far! But why does this lie work so perfectly? It is important to know that this has been prepared for a long time.

Let's start from the root, which hardly anyone approaches, the so-called virus itself. The word virus was introduced by Louis Pasteur and comes from Latin, it means poison.

The word poison in world is neuter, so it is not the virus, but rather the virus. Already here the manipulation begins, because officially the virus is said and written, in order to divert from the origin, thus the word poison, because that could bring up questions.

Now a virus is supposed to be a non-living being, which has neither a cell nucleus, therefore it is not a unicellular organism, and it is supposed to have no metabolism. Nevertheless, such a virus should have genetic information and also protein molecules.

But where is always the genetic information, i.e. the DNA? Correct, in the cell nucleus. But only in unicellular organisms with a cell nucleus, which a virus is not. Let's move on to the protein.

A protein can be formed exclusively only by a complex organism which has a metabolism, that is an irrefutable, biological fact, even a single cell cannot form a protein.

So where does this non-living being called virus get this protein from which it supposedly attacks our cells in order to reproduce itself? So a complete impossibility.

Up to now also nobody has been able to show a virus, all these pretty pictures of alleged viruses are of course fakes. So there is a fraud! Do so-something, then you would be condemned.

By the way all the so-called children's diseases and other diseases have other causes, the facts about it can be requested with pleasure from me.

Since the invention of vaccinations, this virus fairy tale has brought unimaginable profits to the vaccine manufacturers. This fairy tale could hold itself, because also politicians profited from it and today more than ever.

Honest statesmen, who do not play this game, are eliminated, like recently the president of Tanzania.

Did you know, for example, that the German Minister of Health, Jens Georg Spahn, has founded a lobby company for the pharmaceutical industry and is "earning" heavily from this production?

Or did you know that the Bavarian Prime Minister Markus Söder is involved in a company that manufactures these masks and which are then overpriced by taxpayers' money preferentially purchased?

This continues internationally in such a way, it exists no single politician, in prominent position, which does not have financial advantages at this Corona production.

In addition, there are other funds that are provided directly by the pharmaceutical industry, so to speak. A corrupt politician is a good politician, at least for those interested in the continuation of this game.

Already before, the idea of an epidemic was tried out several times, so to speak as a test to see if mankind would follow obediently.

Among other things, this AIDS staging was also such a test. Now AIDS and many other "diseases" obviously no longer exist, now one has Corona.

But already with this AIDS staging people should have noticed that it is just a staging.

A so-called HIV virus was presented in such a way that it supposedly resided exclusively in the abdomen, so to speak, because it was always said that one can drink from the same coffee cup that an AIDS patient uses.

This HIV virus spread exclusively through sexual intercourse, it never left the infected person through any other way, a well-behaved trained virus that is.

Of course, people did not die from an HIV virus, they died from the pharmaceuticals they were given, because these caused a total breakdown of the immune system.

Some celebrities were also sacrificed to make this fairy tale more believable. The so-called AIDS tests, of course, did not look for a virus, because something that does not exist cannot be found.

These tests only detected the presence of cellular residues in the blood, that is, our own components. So if our immune system was working more, this test found more components.

So a crazy paradox, people with a well working immune system were classified as infected with an immune deficiency disease. Could it get any crazier?

Today's Corona tests basically work the same way.

It is about two things, on the one hand it is about turning people into non-thinking consumers in order to generate the greatest possible profits from them, this has succeeded, it is bought and thrown away as if there were no tomorrow.

On the other hand it is already for a long time about the population reduction, because fewer humans can be controlled better and all the Mitesser by administration of the useful cattle, because as that the large-scale industries see humans, become also fewer.

All this began already long time ago. The vaccinations, already of the infants and small children, which were accomplished even as multiple vaccinations, have the only sense to destroy the only developing immune system already in this phase.

The toxic ingredients of the vaccine sera, especially aluminum, destroy especially the neurons in the brain.

The result we see today very clearly, mankind can no longer think logically and rationally, so they do not recognize all the facts.

By the way, in order to be able to determine the state of mental decay perfectly, the face masks were introduced. There could not be a better and more exact test about the mental state, because the masks are very obviously recognizable.

The supposed viruses, of course, enter the body only through the nose and mouth, never through the eyes and ears. Also they do not sit on clothes, not on products, not on money, not on furniture etc. and also the wild animals are not bothered by the viruses.

The further purpose of the masks is an even faster dumbing down of mankind, because through the masks the organism gets too little oxygen, the consequence is an undersupply of the brain and more neurons die.

All in all, a perfect, albeit perfidious plan, which is now working brilliantly.

Why all these "experts" above all biologists, who would know it, play along this fraud?

I had talked to some of them, they say it honestly, namely that otherwise they would lose their job and their career would be over.

Of course this is so and defamations, also with the famous word conspiracy theorist, will follow.

Nevertheless, we can not understand these people, because they obviously do not understand that their own future and especially that of their children is thus sealed.

Perhaps these "experts" are also no longer able to apply this logic.

I do not want to drag out this text too much, although there are many more facts. But anyone interested is welcome to contact me.

We are fighting against these devilish intendants of this spectacle, we have already been able to achieve many successes.

If we stand still, our children will go into a very dark future, if they are "allowed" to live at all, according to the will of these lunatics..

Table of Contents

The start of a dictatorship?

If you believe politics and the mainstream media, the world will return to normal in 2022. The ordered mass vaccinations will help contain the pandemic, we will all be allowed to work and move freely as before, and the economy will recover after the recession of the century.

However, this optimistic scenario is not only unlikely, but unfortunately impossible. The year 2021 marks a decisive turning point in the history of mankind. It has been brought about by the digital-financial complex, headed by the world's largest IT corporations, the asset manager BlackRock and the central banks.

This triumvirate, which has dominated large parts of the world since the turn of the millennium, expanded its power in 2021 in a previously unimaginable way and will certainly continue to work on seizing complete control over humanity in 2022.

The tool the digital-financial complex relies on to do this is scaremongering. Last year, it used a disease as an opportunity to put all of humanity in a state of emergency and to ruthlessly push its own agenda. This is: total control through digitalization and partial privatization of money.

2020 has finally shown that politics, the most influential media and the central banks are nothing more than compliant instruments of domination of the digital-financial complex, whose global power far surpasses anything mankind has ever experienced.

Its rise began in the 1990s. The unstoppable progress of digital technology helped its most important representatives Apple, Microsoft, Google, Amazon and Facebook to a breathtaking triumphal march. At the same time, the progressive deregulation of the financial sector made BlackRock a leading global giant in the field of asset management.

An important historical milestone was the world financial crisis of 2007/2008, since when the global financial system has been kept alive only by central banks. The two largest of them, the U.S. Federal Reserve and the European Central Bank, not only created trillions of dollars out of thin air, but also channeled a large part of it into the pockets of ultra-rich investors with the help of BlackRock.

In this way, a cycle has been created that has ensured a historically unprecedented redistribution of wealth from the bottom to the top. This has been taken to extremes in 2020. Under the pretext of fighting a disease, almost the entire global economy was brought to a standstill in the spring. Then the central banks, with the help of BlackRock, allocated by far the largest sums ever to large investors as supposed bailout money.

The collateral damage of this action: several hundred million people in developing countries have been deprived of their livelihoods, and the number of hungry people has increased by more than 130 million in 2020, according to UN figures.

In addition, economic damage has been caused in the industrialized countries, the devastating consequences of which are yet to be seen. Already foreseeable are the collapse of many small and micro enterprises and the death of a large part of the middle class, mass layoffs in large companies, and an avalanche of credit defaults that will shake the banking system.

As a result of the various lockdowns, government budgets are running the largest deficits ever, so that mass layoffs in the public sector will have to occur and tax increases and drastic cuts in social spending will be unavoidable.

To keep this doomed system alive anyway, all indications are that there will soon be an attempt to end the banking system in its present form and put credit creation exclusively in the hands of the central banks.

For all of us, this means that we must expect a drastic reduction in our standard of living and total control of all areas of life, including our finances. Not only that, but since all these changes are sure to meet with considerable social resistance, we must also expect those in charge to try to further restrict our democratic rights such as freedom of travel, freedom of expression and freedom of assembly, which have already been curtailed in unprecedented ways this year.

The year that began last Friday will thus present us all with a historic alternative: It will either lock us definitively into a global prison dominated by the digital-financial complex, or we will rise up against this modern form of slavery to take up the fight for a self-determined life.

There is no third way.

The Great Depression 2022?

We are inching ever closer to the mother of all economic depressions and its effects are about to cause an unprecedented amount of turbulence, chaos and despair in our modern society. The horror stories of the Great Depression of the 1930s are about to repeat themselves. Most preppers have that grim era burned into their minds as a stark reminder of how quickly things can go wrong, even in the richest country in the world. And today, global events are accelerating rapidly and things are spiraling out of control at an alarming rate in the United States.

For decades, preppers had the Great Depression as a motivation and reminder to prepare for dark times even before things started going bad. But the truth is, this is the scenario we should all be preparing for. Recently, a number of economists, financial analysts and market watchers have warned that another Great Depression is coming that will return us to an era of poverty, hunger and distress that will likely begin later this year. Last year, when the healthcare crisis hit the U.S., the economy fell into a deep recession in a matter of days. More than 700,000 jobless claims were filed in a few months and U.S. GDP fell 31.4% in the second quarter, the deepest and fastest collapse ever recorded.

However, due to the extraordinary amount of printed money artificially injected into the system by the Federal Reserve, our economy has gone numb. These measures may have prevented a major collapse in the short term, but they created huge imbalances that now threaten to bring down the entire system. Every dollar of those government stimulus checks was created out of thin air by the Fed or borrowed from the Treasury. At some point, the consequences of having expanded our money supply by trillions would start knocking on our doors. So now we are facing an inflationary spike the likes of which we have not seen in modern times.

To make matters worse, the price of essential goods, such as housing, has soared to record highs, so Americans now have to spend much more money to buy or rent a home. This also contributes to a weaker dollar and even more persistent inflation. As our currency degrades, we have to pay more for imported goods, such as oil.

Consequently, gasoline prices are bound to rise, and car prices also become more expensive because we import many cars from other countries.

Given the strong imbalances between supply and demand, prices are rising mercilessly all over the world. Companies have to pay more for energy and raw materials, so they pass these costs on to consumers. Rising gas prices and transportation costs also add to consumer prices. Therefore, even though we now have more dollars in the economy, our purchasing power has diminished considerably. Once inflation infiltrates the system, it begins to feed on itself and takes off like a rocket.

Since the Fed intervened with its monetary policies, our money supply has begun to inflate by about $1 billion per hour. On the other hand, our national debt is increasing so rapidly that it is hard to keep track of it. By 2030, interest on the debt is expected to equal and then exceed tax revenues. That means we will have to borrow and print more money to pay the interest on the money we borrowed and printed during the last recession. No wonder many economists say our economic system will collapse much sooner. All of this is making inflation worse, and it may be too late for the government to get the situation back under control. The smart ones will be prepared in advance for the Great Depression looming on the horizon.

The Depression of the 1930s did a lot of damage to our country, but the next crisis will be much, much worse. Today our economy is much more interconnected, and if America goes down, the rest of the world will suffer as well. No one will come to our rescue, especially now that all the major economies are experiencing continuous disruptions. Have you ever imagined what a world without enough energy for everyone would be like? Or without enough food? Have you ever thought about what you will have to do to survive in a world of limited resources? Because that's what you should start thinking about right now. This is going to be our future, and most people are still unaware of the risks and threats ahead of us. But we've been warned. So the only question that remains is: Are you prepared?

Blame China?

It has become common practice in the alternative media to blame China and the Chinese Communist Party for just about everything. Many of these alternative blogs place the blame for Covid-19 related actions on the Chinese Communist Party of the People's Republic of China - especially a sector of blogs that provide detailed, and often quite accurate, data on how COVID-19 "vaccines" are used to wipe out the population and on the massive frauds engineered by corporate elites using the United Nations and the World Health Organization.

In some cases, the conclusion of these reports is that the U.S. is under assault by the Communists of China and that the U.S. Democrats who go along with their treasonous acts are "leftists."

Concern about the actions of the Chinese Communist Party CCP in the United States, and globally, is not without evidence.

There are examples of powerful business interests, and super-rich, in China using the authority of the Chinese Communist Party to advance their interests. However, the simplistic and reductive manner in which crimes committed by corporate elites and billionaires in the United States are attributed to the CCP, and the way in which attention is diverted away from "the real sources of evil," which are American, suggests that we are dealing with a carefully organized disinformation campaign, most likely funded by the financial elites of Goldman Sachs, BlackRock, Morgan Stanley, etc.

The objective of attacking the CCP is to mislead, to prevent us from identifying the enemy within. Well known brands like Microsoft, Coca Cola, Facebook, Oracle, Walmart and Amazon are the main source of the rampant criminal policies at home that are turning the nation into a concentration camp.

These companies are the playthings of the superrich, who do their deals, sometimes also with Chinese elites, behind closed doors.

In short, this psychological operation of blaming the Chinese Communist Party is aimed at delaying the realization among citizens of the bitter reality of fascism at home until the last possible moment and concealing the growth of a radical class society.

The exaggeration of the "Chinese threat" is a diversion concocted by the super-rich. The aim is to get people frothing at the mouth about foreigners from an alien civilization and thus unable to understand the conspiracy of the rich to destroy the lives of ordinary people.

The vast majority of information about the political actions of corporate interests, under the cloak of government, in the United States, China, Russia, Israel,

Turkey, Germany, Japan and other great powers, is classified and completely inaccessible to ordinary citizens. We must first understand how little we know.

However, focusing exclusively on the CCP makes no one seriously ask who are the important foreign powers, besides China, in DC. Moreover, citizens assume that Facebook, Amazon and Microsoft are "American" companies, even as those criminal organizations conspire to tear America apart.

Most bloggers who talk about geopolitics limit themselves to sensationalist stories created for public consumption and can't even mention the possibility that Chinese and American elites have created a fake cold war to block meaningful dialogue between ordinary citizens and increase their profits.

Such obliviousness is not accidental. Those self-styled experts refuse to address the class issue.

The Chinese Communist Party (CCP) is a massive institution that is part of the government of the People's Republic of China and represents, in theory, the people.

Previously, the CCP was strictly regulated. However, over the past 20 years it has been deregulated and large sections of the organization are now run like the Lions Club. Large sections of the CCP form a network of powerful people who pursue benefits for their friends and family, and do not function as a government agency.

This is no secret to the Chinese and there are demands for reform at home, and serious efforts.

There are also factions within the CCP that want to revive the party traditions of the 1940s and 1950s, to stand with the workers, not the multinational banks. Their numbers are growing.

The Democratic Party and the Republican Party are worse than the CCP in the sense that they make national policy behind closed doors, but their role is not defined by the Constitution and they are not a responsible part of the government.

There are specific objectives behind the corporate media push, and conservative blogs, that cast CCP as the bad guy to distract attention from institutional decay in the United States.

1) Deviously attributing the loss of freedom and the intentional destruction of the U.S. economy to "communism" and "leftism" rather than corporate fascism that is the fruit of American finance.

Intentionally labeling "corporate fascism" as "communism" and attributing the criminal plans of U.S. CEOs to a devious CCP belonging to an alien civilization is an orchestrated psy-op at the highest level that reinvents the "Yellow Peril" mythologies that dominated America in the 19th century as a tool of political control.

2) The projection of rampant criminality into China, and away from Washington D.C., through the creation of a drama dominated by an alien and mysterious CCP serves to obscure how close evil is to the United States.

It obscures the criminality born of familiar American brand names like Amazon, Facebook, Bank of America, Coca Cola, Walmart and Microsoft, and even encourages Americans to embrace these dangerous foreign entities as "American" corporations in response to a supposed Chinese threat.

But these multinational corporations have no more right to testify in Congress and lobby than the CCP. They provide benefits to the superrich, men who know no country, and shareholders around the world.

3) The demonization of the CCP is supported by the military-industrial complex because this invented existential threat is central to the establishment of a war economy in the United States that assumes there will be a war with China.

As the U.S. economy sinks into anomie as a result of radical deregulation of finance, a war economy is increasingly perceived as salvation. Ensuring that the war economy is run through the Pentagon ensures that multinational corporations get a thick slice of the pie.

In addition, the decline of the judiciary, legislature and executive in the U.S. has created an environment in which the military has an increasingly important role because it is the only part of government that remains partially functional.

4) It is fundamental to the "new cold war" that no discourse is possible between ordinary Chinese and Americans, that no alliances can be established between concerned citizens in both countries, that no conversations can take place between intellectuals in the two countries.

If citizens were to talk to citizens, they could discover how multinational corporations are pitting Chinese and American workers against each other as they proceed to destroy the economies of both countries.

5) The attack on the CCP and Democratic Party "leftists" found in the conservative alternative media serves to brand the term such as "communism," "socialism," and "leftism" as negatives in the public imagination that are falsely associated with the social and economic consequences of the policies of "corporate fascism."

How the U.S. Communist Party led the battle for civil rights, and the left fought for many of the benefits workers enjoy today, is intentionally obscured in these anti-left campaigns that link "socialism" to a threatening Chinese culture.

6) Perhaps the most devious game of all is to force Americans to choose an anti-left and anti-Chinese (and by extension anti-Asian) ideology if they want to find a voice critical of the COVID-19 regime.

The "leftists" in the media are pro-vaccine and the only opposition to vaccines we see are Donald Biden supporters. This political configuration makes it possible for liberals and progressives to dismiss the obvious dangers of vaccines without fear of backlash.

7) Blaming everything on a sneaky CCP is an underhanded way to avoid any serious analysis of who owns what in America and what the real implications of wealth concentration have been for ordinary people.

If citizens knew how these billionaires made their vast fortunes, not through innovation and imagination, but by stealing cash from the Federal Reserve that belongs to the nation's citizens, and creating inflation that punishes citizens, they would be calling for those billionaires to be jailed.

Blaming it on a vague CCP that is beyond the comprehension of citizens helps people avoid any discussion of who owns what, and how they got hold of it.

There are examples of corruption and influence peddling involving the Chinese Communist Party. That part of the story is true. But the ultimate goal of the demonization of the CCP is clearly not to reduce foreign influence in Washington D.C. (which is skyrocketing these days), but to find a convenient and misguided way to explain the deep moral corruption of American society.

The goal of the demonization of the CCP is not to reduce foreign influence in Washington D.C. (which is skyrocketing these days), but to find a convenient and misguided way to explain the deep moral corruption of American society.

The roots of the great reset

Propaganda disseminated by Anglo-American intelligence has led many to believe that the Communist Party of China is the root of the Great Reset (a.k.a. Great Reset) agenda. However, this perception is far removed from reality.

In this revealing chapter, we traced the roots of the Great Reset agenda eighty years ago, when James Burnham - an American Oxford University graduate, a false-flag Trotskyist who later joined the OSS and CIA and who became the founding father of neoconservatism - wrote his worldview in "The Managers' Revolution." Chung claims that it was the ideologies of Burnham's "The Managers' Revolution" that led Orwell to write his work "1984."

As Orwell said in his essay "Secondary Thoughts on Burnham:" "It will be seen that Burnham's theory is not, strictly speaking, a new theory. Many earlier writers have foreseen the emergence of a new type of society, neither capitalist nor socialist, and probably based on slavery..."

Either way, James Burnham's ideas correspond to the Malthusian zero-growth paradigm planned by the Anglo-Venetian aristocracy and the new American elites, and their Great Reset towards oligarchic collectivism. According to a 2013 UK government white paper: alumni who studied in the UK are encouraged to form "networks of people in positions of influence around the world who can promote British foreign policy objectives," similar to discrete societies such as Freemasonry.

Klaus Schwab, the architect of the World Economic Forum founded in 1971 - one of the leading, if not the leading, influencer and funder of what will set the course for global economic policy outside of governments - has been the cause of much concern and suspicion since he announced the "Great Reset" agenda at the 50th annual meeting of the World Economic Forum (WEF) in June 2020.

The initiative The Great Reset is a somewhat vague call for the need for global stakeholders to coordinate a simultaneous "management" of the effects of COVID-19 on the global economy, which they have disturbingly dubbed "pandenomics." This, we are told, will be the new normal, the new reality to which we will have to adjust in the immediate future.

It should be known that, almost from its inception, the World Economic Forum aligned itself with the Club of Rome, a think tank of aristocrats and elite members, founded in 1968, to address the problems of humanity. In its extremely influential work "The Limits to Growth," published in 1972, the Club of Rome concluded that these problems could not be solved on their own and that they were all interrelated. In 1991, the co-founder of the Club of Rome, Sir Alexander King, stated in "The

27

First Global Revolution" (an evaluation of the first 30 years of the Club of Rome) that the enemy of humanity is mankind itself:

"In looking for a common enemy against which we could unite, it occurred to us that pollution, the threat of global warming, water shortages, famine and the like, would fit together. Taken together and in their interactions, these phenomena constitute a common threat that we must all face together. But in designating these dangers as the enemy, we fall into the trap, of which we have already warned readers, of confusing symptoms with causes. All these dangers are caused by human intervention in natural processes, and only through a change in attitudes and behaviors can they be overcome. The real enemy, then, is humanity itself."

Not surprisingly, with such a conclusion, part of the prescribed solution was the need for population control.

However, what forms of population control was Klaus Schwab thinking of in particular?

In the late 1960s, Schwab attended Harvard and among his professors was Sir Henry Kissinger, whom he has described as one of the figures who most influenced his thinking throughout his life.

[Henry Kissinger and his former student, Klaus Schwab, welcome former British Prime Minister Ted Heath at the

1980 WEF annual meeting. Source: World Economic Forum]

To get a better idea of the kind of influence Sir Henry Kissinger exerted on the young Klaus Schwab, we should take a look at Kissinger's infamous report NSSM-200: Implications of World Population Growth for U.S. Security and Interests Abroad(img), also known as "The Kissinger Report," published in 1974. This report, declassified in 1989, was instrumental in transforming U.S. foreign policy from pro-development/pro-industry to promoting underdevelopment through totalitarian methods in support of population control. Kissinger states the following in the report:

"... if future figures are to be kept within reasonable limits, it is urgent that fertility reduction measures in the 1970s and 1980s be initiated and made effective ... [Financial] aid will be given to other countries, taking into account such factors as population growth ... Food and agricultural aid is vital to any population-sensitive development strategy ... Allocation of scarce resources should take into account the steps a country is taking in population control ... There is an alternative view that compulsory programs may be necessary ..."

For Kissinger, the U.S. foreign policy orientation was wrong in its emphasis on ending hunger by providing the means of industrial and scientific development to poor nations, according to Kissinger, such an initiative would only lead to greater global imbalance as the new middle classes would consume more, and waste strategic resources.

In the "Essay on the Principle of Population" (1799), Thomas Malthus wrote:

"We should facilitate, instead of foolishly and vainly endeavoring to prevent, the operations of nature in the production of this mortality; and if we fear the too frequent visitation of the horrible form of famine, we should sedulously encourage the other forms of destruction, which we compel nature to use. In our cities we should make the streets narrower, crowd more people into houses, and court the return of pestilence."

As a staunch Malthusian, Kissinger believed that "nature" had provided the means to cull the herd, and through the use of economic policies that utilized the courtship of plague, famine and so forth, they were simply enforcing a natural hierarchy that was necessary for global stability.

In addition to this extremely disturbing ideology that is one step away from eugenics, there has also been a great deal of disturbance over the 2016 World Economic Forum video reviewing their 8 "predictions" for how the world will change by 2030, with the slogan "You will own nothing, and you will be happy."

It is this particular slogan that has probably caused the most panic among the average citizen wondering what the outcome of the Great Reset will look like. It has also caused much confusion as to who or what is at the root of shaping this mysterious, Orwellian prediction of the future.

Many have come to believe that the root of this agenda is the Communist Party of China. However, whatever your opinion of the Chinese government and President Xi's intentions, the roots of the Great Reset agenda can be traced very clearly to 80 years ago, when James Burnham - an American former Trotskyist who later joined the OSS, the CIA, and later became the founding father of neoconservatism, wrote a book about his vision of "The Managers' Revolution."

In fact, it was the ideologies of Burnham's "The Managers' Revolution" that led Orwell to write his "1984".

The true founder

"James Burnham is the true intellectual founder of the neoconservative movement and the original proselytizer, in the United States, of the theory of 'totalitarianism'." - **Christopher Hitchens**, "For the Sake of Argument: Essay and Minority Reports."

Understandably, there is some confusion as to how a former high-profile Trotskyist became the founder of the neoconservative movement. However, the truth of the matter is that Burnham was neither.

That is, James Burnham never changed his beliefs and convictions at any point during his journey through Trotskyism, OSS/CIA intelligence and neoconservatism, although he may have backstabbed many along the way, and this two-part series will review why this is so.

James Burnham was born in 1905 in Chicago, Illinois, and was raised Roman Catholic, but later rejected Catholicism while studying at Princeton and professed atheism for the rest of his life until shortly before his death, when he reportedly returned to the church. (1) He would graduate from Princeton, followed by Balliol College at Oxford University and in 1929 become a professor of philosophy at New York University.

It was during this period that Burnham met Sidney Hook, who was also a professor of philosophy at NYU, and who in his autobiography boasted of having converted Burnham to Marxism. In 1933, along with Sidney Hook, Burnham helped organize the socialist organization American Workers Party (AWP).

It would not be long before Burnham found Trotsky's use of "dialectical materialism" to explain the interplay between human and historical forces in his "History of the Russian Revolution" brilliant. As founder of the Red Army, Trotsky had dedicated his life to the spread of a world communist revolution, which Stalin opposed with Trotsky's ideology of "Permanent Revolution." In this ideology, the Trotskyists were tactically trained to be militant experts in infighting, infiltration and disorganization.

Among these tactics was "entryism," in which one organization encourages its members to join another, often larger, organization in an attempt to take over that organization or convert a large part of its membership with its own ideology and directive.

The best known example of this technique was called the French Turn, when French Trotskyists in 1934 infiltrated the Section Francaise de l'International Ouvriere (SFIO, French Socialist Party) with the intention of recruiting the most militant elements.

That same year, the Trotskyists of the Communist League of America (CLA) made a French turn to the American Workers Party, in a move that elevated James

Burnham of the AWP to the role of Trotsky's top lieutenant and adviser.

Burnham would continue the tactics of infiltration and subversion of other left-wing parties and in 1935 attempted to make a French turn in the much larger Socialist Party (SP), however, in 1937, the Trotskyists were expelled from the Socialist Party, leading to the formation of the Socialist Workers Party (SWP) at the end of the year. He would resign from the SWP in April 1940 and form the Workers Party, only to resign less than two months later.

Burnham remained a "Trotskyist intellectual" from 1934 to 1940, using militant Trotskyist tactics against competing Marxist movements, flipping their loyalties and plundering their best talents. Although Burnham worked six years for the Trotskyists, at the beginning of the new decade, he completely renounced both Trotsky and the "philosophy of Marxism," dialectical materialism.

Perhaps Burnham was aware that the walls were closing in on Trotsky, and that it would only be a matter of six months from Burnham's first renunciation that Trotsky would be assassinated in August 1940, in his compound outside Mexico City.

In February 1940 Burnham wrote "Science and Style: A Reply to Comrade Trotsky," in which he broke with dialectical materialism, stressing the importance of

Bertrand Russell's work and Alfred North Whitehead's approach:

"Would you like me to prepare a reading list, Comrade Trotsky? It would be long, going from the work of the brilliant mathematicians and logicians of the middle of the last century to a climax in Russell and Whitehead's monumental Principia Mathematica (the historical turning point in modern logic), and then extending in many directions - one of the most fruitful represented by the scientists, mathematicians and logicians now cooperating in the new Encyclopedia of Unified Science."

On May 21, 1940, Burnham thus summarized his feelings in a letter of resignation from the Labor Party:

"I reject, as you know, the 'philosophy of Marxism,' dialectical materialism. ..."

The general Marxian theory of 'universal history,' insofar as it has any empirical content, seems to me to be refuted by modern historical and anthropological research.

Marxian economics seems to me, for the most part, false or obsolete or meaningless in its application to contemporary economic phenomena. Those aspects of Marxian economics that retain their validity do not seem to me to justify the theoretical structure of economics.

Not only do I think it is meaningless to say that 'socialism is inevitable' and false that socialism is 'the only alternative to capitalism'; I consider that on the basis of the evidence now available to us a new form of exploitative society (which I call 'managerial society') is not only possible but a more likely outcome of the present than socialism. ...

Therefore, I cannot recognize, nor do I feel, any ties or allegiance to the Workers Party (or any other Marxist party) on ideological, theoretical or political grounds. That is simply the way it is, and I can no longer pretend about it, either to myself or to others."

In 1941, Burnham would publish "The Managers' Revolution: What's Happening in the World," which brought him fame and fortune, and was listed by Henry Luce's Life magazine as one of the 100 most outstanding books of 1924-1944.

The managerial revolution

"We cannot understand the revolution by restricting our analysis to the war [World War II]; we must understand the war as a phase in the development of the revolution." - **James Burnham** "The Managerial Revolution."

In "The Managerial Revolution," Burnham argues that if socialism were possible, it would have occurred as a result of the Bolshevik Revolution, but what occurred instead was neither a reversion to a capitalist system nor a transition to a socialist system, but rather the formation of a new organizational structure composed of an elite managerial class, the type of society he believed was in the process of replacing capitalism on a global scale.

Burnham argues that just as the transition from a feudal to a capitalist state is inevitable, so too will the transition from a capitalist to a managerial state occur. And that property rights to production capabilities will no longer be owned by individuals, but by the state or institutions, he writes:

"Effective class domination and privilege require, it is true, the control of the instruments of production; but this need not be exercised through individual private property rights. It may be done through what may be called corporate rights, possessed not by individuals as such, but by institutions: as was the case in many societies in which a priestly class was dominant..."

Burnham proceeds to write:

"If, in an administrative society, no individual should possess comparable property rights, how can a group of individuals constitute a ruling class?

The answer is comparatively simple and, as already noted, is not without historical analogues. The managers will exercise their control over the instruments of production and obtain preference in the distribution of the products, not directly, through the property rights to which they are entitled as individuals, but indirectly, through their control of the State which, in turn, will own and control the instruments of production. The State - that is, the institutions that make up the State - will be, if we want to put it this way, the 'property' of the managers. And that will be enough to place them in the position of the ruling class."

Burnham admits that the ideologies needed to facilitate this transition have not yet been fully worked out, but goes on to say that they can be approached:

"from several different but similar directions, for example: Leninism-Stalinism; Fascism-Nazism; and, at a more primitive level, by the New Deal and by less influential American ideologies [at the time] such as

'technocracy.' This, then, is the skeleton of the theory, expressed in the language of the struggle for power."

This is admittedly a rather confusing paragraph, but it becomes clearer when we understand it from Burnham's specific point of view. As Burnham sees it, all of these different ways are methods of achieving his vision of a managerial society because each way stresses the importance of the state as the central coordinating power, and that such a state will be governed by its "managers." Burnham considers the different moral implications in each scenario irrelevant, since, as he makes clear at the beginning of his book, he has chosen to detach himself from such questions.

Burnham goes on to explain that the support of the masses is necessary for the success of any revolution, which is why the masses must be made to believe that they will benefit from such a revolution, when in reality it is only a matter of replacing one ruling class with another and nothing changes for the underdog. He explains that this is the case with the dream of a socialist state, that the universal equality promised by socialism is just a fairy tale that the people are told to fight for the establishment of a new ruling class, then told that achieving a socialist state will take many decades, and that essentially, a managerial system must be established in the meantime.

Burnham argues that this is what happened in both Nazi Germany and Bolshevik Russia:

"However, it may still turn out that the new form of economy may be called 'socialist.' In the nations-Russia and Germany-that have made the most progress toward the new [entrepreneurial] economy, the term 'socialism' or 'national socialism' is the one commonly used. The motivation for this terminology is not, of course, the desire for scientific clarity, quite the contrary. The word 'socialism' is used for ideological purposes to manipulate the favorable emotions of the masses attached to the historic socialist ideal of a free, classless, international society and to conceal the fact that managerial economics is in reality the basis of a new type of exploitative, class-based society."

Burnham continues:

"The nations- 'Bolshevik' Russia, 'Nazi' Germany, and 'Fascist' Italy-that have moved most toward the managerial social structure are all, at the present time, totalitarian dictatorships...what distinguishes totalitarian dictatorship is the number of facets of life subject to the impact of dictatorial rule. It is not only political actions, in the strictest sense, but almost all aspects of life, business, art, science, education, religion, recreation and morality are not only influenced by the totalitarian regime, but are directly subject to it.

It should be noted that a dictatorship of the totalitarian type would not have been possible in any era prior to our own. Totalitarianism presupposes the development

*of modern technology, especially rapid communication
and transportation. Without the latter, no government,
regardless of its intentions, would have had at its
disposal the physical means to coordinate so intimately
so many aspects of life. Without rapid transportation
and communication, it was relatively easy for people to
keep many aspects of their lives out of the reach of
government. This is no longer possible, or is only
possible to a much lesser degree, when governments
today make deliberate use of the possibilities of modern
technology."*

Orwell & Burnham

Burnham would go on to assert in his "Managerial Revolution" that the Russian Revolution, World War I and its aftermath, the Treaty of Versailles, provided the final proof that capitalist world politics could no longer function and had come to an end. He described World War I as the last war of the capitalists and World War II as the first, but not the last, of the managerial society. Burnham made it clear that many more wars would have to be fought after World War II before the managerial society could finally become fully entrenched.

This continued warfare would lead to the destruction of sovereign nation states, such that only a small number of large nations would survive, culminating in the nuclei of three "superstates," which Burnham predicted would center on the United States, Germany, and Japan. He goes on to predict that these superstates will never be able to conquer the other and will be at permanent war until some unforeseeable time. He predicts that Russia will split in two, with the West joining the German sphere and the East joining the Japanese. (Note that this book was published in 1941, so Burnham was clearly of the opinion that Nazi Germany and Fascist Japan would be the victors of World War II).

Burnham states that "sovereignty will be limited to the few superstates."

In fact, he goes so far as to state at the beginning of his book that the managerial revolution is not a prediction of something that will occur in the future, it is something that has already begun and is, in fact, in its final stages of becoming, that it has already been successfully implemented around the world and that the battle is essentially over.

The National Review, founded by James Burnham and William F. Buckley (more on this in part two), wants to put the veneer that although Orwell was critical of Burnham's views, he was ultimately creatively inspired to write about it in his novel "1984." Yes, inspired is one way of putting it, or more accurately, that he was appalled by Burnham's views and wrote his novel as a stark warning of what would ultimately be the result of such monstrous theorizations, which to this day would organize the zeitgeist of thought to be suspicious of anything resembling such neologisms as "Big Brother," "Thought Police," "Two Minutes of Hate," "Room 101," "memory hole," "Newspeak," "doublethink," "unperson," "thoughtcrime," and "groupthink."

George Orwell, (whose real name is Eric Arthur Blair), first published his "Second Thoughts on James Burnham" in May 1946. The novel "1984" would be published in 1949.

In his essay he dissects Burnham's proposed ideology outlined in "The Managerial Revolution" and "The Machiavellians. Defenders of Liberty."

Orwell writes:

"It is clear that Burnham is fascinated by the spectacle of power, and that his sympathies were with Germany as long as Germany appeared to be winning the war...Curiously enough, when one examines the predictions which Burnham has based on his general theory, one finds that, in so far as they are verifiable, they have been falsified...It will be seen that Burnham's predictions have not only proved wrong, when they were verifiable, but have sometimes been sensationally contradicted.... Political predictions are often wrong, because they are usually based on wishful thinking...Often the telling factor is the date at which they are made...It will be seen that at every moment Burnham is predicting a continuation of what is happening...The tendency to do this is not merely a bad habit, like inaccuracy or exaggeration...It is a major mental disease, and its roots lie partly in cowardice and partly in the cult of power, which is not entirely separable from cowardice.....

The cult of power clouds political judgment because it leads, almost inevitably, to the belief that current trends will continue. Whoever wins at the time will always seem invincible. If the Japanese have conquered South Asia, they will hold South Asia forever, if the Germans have captured Tobruk, they will unfailingly capture Cairo... The rise and fall of empires, the disappearance of cultures and religions, are expected to occur with the rapidity of an earthquake, and processes that have barely begun are spoken of as if they were already at an end. Burnham's writings are full of apocalyptic visions... Within the space of five years Burnham predicted the domination of Russia by Germany and of Germany by Russia. In each case he obeyed the same instinct: the instinct to bow to the conqueror of the moment, to accept the existing tendency as irreversible."

Interestingly, and fortunately, we hear that George Orwell does not take Burnham's predictions of a managerial revolution as immovable, but that he has shown himself in a short period of time too full of illusions and bent on worshipping the power of the moment. However, this does not mean that we should not pay attention to the orchestrations of these madmen.

The start of the Great Reset?

Burnham made it clear in this book that not only was he quite willing to accept the outcome of a victorious Nazi Germany (this was his conclusion at the time), but that this was a natural and inevitable course that the whole world would have no choice but to follow. Burnham had no qualms about regarding Nazi Germany as the highest form of his concept of "managerial society."

In his work "The Managerial Revolution" he claimed that the Russian Revolution, World War I and its aftermath, and the Treaty of Versailles were the ultimate proof that capitalist world politics could no longer function and had come to an end. He described World War I as the last war of the capitalists and World War II as the first, but not the last, of the managerial society. And that after World War II many more wars would have to be fought before the managerial society could finally become fully established.

This continuing war would lead to the destruction of sovereign nation states, such that only a small number of large nations would survive, culminating in the nuclei of three "superstates," which Burnham predicted would center on the United States, Germany and Japan. He went on to predict that these superstates would never be able to conquer the other and would be at permanent war until some unforeseeable time.

He predicted that Russia would split in two, incorporating the west into the German sphere and the east into the Japanese. (Note that this book was published in 1941, so Burnham was clearly of the opinion that Nazi Germany and Fascist Japan would be the victors of World War II). Burnham states that "sovereignty will be limited to the few superstates."

This future of "eternal wars" among a few superstates has obvious remnant influences of Trotsky's militant "Permanent Revolution" ideology.

This was also just the sort of thing Allen Dulles was talented at pursuing.

During the 1920s and 1930s, both Dulles brothers acted as major players in the "rearmament of Germany by night," organized largely through their law firm Sullivan & Cromwell, which functioned as the hub of an intricate international network of banks, investment firms, and industrial conglomerates that helped rebuild Germany after World War I. The Dulles brothers' German representative in the law firm was a key player in the "rearmament of Germany by night.

The German representative of the Dulles brothers' firm was Dr. Gerhardt Alois Westrick, who acted simultaneously as Hitler's financial agent and as the Abwehr's chief of espionage in the United States. In January 1940, Westrick received the title of Wehrwirtschaftsführer for his contributions to the war effort. He was then assigned by von Ribbentrop to a mission to the United States to meet with American business leaders and gain their support for Germany.

Allen Dulles was also a director of the J. Henry Schroder Bank, whose German president, SS General Baron Kurt von Schroder, was one of Schacht's chief aides in organizing the fund that financed Hitler's rise to power in 1933. Allen Dulles remained on the board of directors of the Schroder Bank until 1944, long after taking up his post as head of the OSS in Switzerland.

Allen Dulles also worked closely with Thomas McKittrick, an old Wall Street crony who was president of the Bank for International Settlements. Five of its directors would later be indicted for war crimes, among them Hermann Schmitz, one of Dulles' many BIS-related law clients. Schmitz was the CEO of IG Farben, the chemical conglomerate that became famous for its production of Zyklon B, the gas used in Hitler's death camps, and for its extensive use of slave labor during the war.

David Talbot writes in his work The Devil's Chessboard:

"The secretive Bank for International Settlements became a crucial financial partner for the Nazis. Emil Puhl - vice-president of Hitler's Reichsbank and close associate of McKittrick - once called the BIS the only 'foreign branch' of the Reichsbank. The Bank for International Settlements laundered hundreds of millions of dollars in Nazi gold looted from the treasuries of the occupied countries."

Allen Dulles was first recruited into the OSS (Office of Strategic Services) in October 1941, a sort of precursor to the CIA. For most of his OSS work he was stationed in Bern, Switzerland, where it was later discovered that he was involved in a number of incredibly suspicious activities that would lead one to suspect that his loyalties and allegiances were indeed with Nazi Germany.

Such activities included sabotaging the success of U.S. intelligence operations and engaging in secret negotiations on behalf of individuals directly or indirectly affiliated with the Nazi Party, one of the best known incidents of this being Dulles' curious conduct during Operation Sunrise, also known as the Bern incident, on behalf of SS General Kurt Wolff.

[In a previous article in the three-part series I go over more details of the fascist roots of the CIA, and how Allen Dulles, and his brother Foster Dulles, play instrumental roles in all of this].

The Office of Policy Coordination (OPC) was created as a department of the CIA in 1948, but functioned as a clandestine operation until October 1950. Many of the agency's recruits were "former" Nazis.

The OPC was preceded by the Special Procedures Group (SPG), whose creation in March 1948 had been authorized in December 1947 with President Harry Truman's approval of the top-secret policy document NSC 4-A.

NSC 4-A was a new directive to cover "clandestine paramilitary operations, as well as political and economic warfare", this provided the authorization for CIA intervention in the Italian elections of April 1948 (in favor of Italy's Christian Democracy, which was hiding thousands of Fascists in its ranks, as opposed to what would have been the election of the Communist Party of Italy, which was admired for leading the fight against Mussolini). This success in manipulating the Italian elections proved that psychological/political warfare could be the key to "winning" the Cold War.

When the OPC was created, it inherited all the resources of the SPG.

On June 18, 1948, NSC 4-A was replaced by NSC 10/2, creating the Office of Political Coordination (OPC). NSC 10/2 was the first presidential document to specify a mechanism for approving and managing covert operations, and also the first to define the term "covert operations."

George F. Kennan, director of the State Department's Policy Planning Staff, was the key figure in the creation of the OPC. Frank Wisner, who worked as a Wall Street lawyer for the law firm of Carter, Ledyard & Milburn, was a former member of the OSS and very close to Allen Dulles. He would be called from the State Department as the first director of the TPO.

From 1948 to 1950, the OPC, although technically a department within the CIA, was not under CIA control, but was a renegade operation run by Allen Dulles and Frank Wisner. The OPC came under CIA control in October 1950, when Walter Bedell Smith became Director of Central Intelligence, and it was renamed the Directorate of Plans (for more on this, see my article).

During the 1948-1950 period, Dulles and Wisner were essentially operating their own private spy agency, probably with the special blessing of George F. Kennan, since the OPC was actually more beholden to the State Department than to the CIA during this period.

During World War II, Burnham left his teaching position at New York University to work for the OSS and continued to work for the CIA when the OSS was disbanded in September 1945. He would later be recommended by George F. Kennan to head the semi-autonomous "Psychological Strategy Board" (PSB) division of the Office of Policy Coordination (OPC).

This is no coincidence, as the American-Jewish author Naomi Wiener Cohen states in her book "Jacob H. Schiff: A Study in American Jewish Leadership" about the disastrous effects for Russia of the British-inspired

Russo-Japanese war (February 1904 to September 1905), which brought about the Russian "revolution" of 1905, which lasted until 1907. That revolution paved the way for the overthrow of the Tsar and the coming to power of the Bolsheviks in the October Revolution of 1917:

"The Russo-Japanese war allied Schiff with George Kennan in an enterprise to spread revolutionary propaganda among Russian prisoners of war held by Japan (Kennan had access to them). The operation was a carefully guarded secret and was not publicly revealed by Kennan until the revolution of March 1917. He then told how he had obtained Japanese permission to visit the camps and how the prisoners had asked him for something to read. By getting the "Friends of Russian Freedom" to send a ton of revolutionary material, he secured Schiff's financial support. As Kennan recounted, fifty thousand officers and men returned to Russia [as] ardent revolutionaries. There they became fifty thousand 'seeds of freedom' in one hundred regiments that contributed to the overthrow of the czar."

Thus, it can be argued that George Kennan brought Burnham in, specifically because of his history as an experienced senior Trotskyist, and because of his, as Orwell says, willingness to worship the power of the moment and his conviction that ultimate power could only be achieved through a "permanent revolution."

George Kennan was also not an ideological socialist, best known as the author of the Cold War "containment" strategy, adamantly opposed FDR's recognition of the Soviet Union, refused to support the United States collaborating with the Soviets in defeating Hitler, accusing Stalin of being just as bad...or perhaps he preferred Hitler's succession to power?

Kennan writes in his Memoirs:

"We should have no relationship with them 'the Soviets'...I never - neither then nor later - considered the Soviet Union a suitable ally or partner, actual or potential, for this country."

Kennan made it clear that he was not an admirer of Stalin's Soviet Union, but he certainly thought differently about the uses of the "old" Trotskyist militants, possibly it was this branch of the Bolsheviks that he really wanted to see succeed? Perhaps they were going to play a similar role for subversion from within in the United States as they did in Russia?

As Paul Fitzgerald and Elizabeth Gould say in their excellent article "How the CIA Created a False Western Reality for Unconventional Warfare":

"Burnham functioned as a critical connection between Wisner's office and the intelligentsia moving from the far left to the far right with ease. Burnham found in Congress a place to denounce not only communism but

also the noncommunist left and left many wondering whether his views were not as dangerous to liberal democracy as communism."

According to Frances Stoner Saunders [author of the acclaimed book "The Cultural Cold War"], members of the British delegation felt that the rhetoric coming out of the congress was a deeply troubling sign of what was to come... "I felt, well, these are the same people who seven years ago were probably howling in the same way at Dr. Goebbels' similar denunciations of communism at the Sports Palast. And I felt, well, what kind of people are we identifying with? That was what shocked me the most. There was a moment during the Congress when I felt we were being invited to invoke Beelzebub to defeat Stalin."

The Congress for Cultural Freedom did not need Beelzebub. It already had him in the form of Burnham, 'Sidney' Hook and Wisner, and in 1952, the party was just getting started... In 1953 Burnham was called back by Wisner to go beyond communism and help overthrow the democratically elected Mohamed Mossadegh in Tehran, Iran... His book, "The Machiavellians: Defenders of Freedom," would become the CIA manual for displacing Western culture with an alternative doctrine for endless conflict in a world of oligarchs. "

The Machiavellians: Burnham's 'managerial' defenders of liberty.

"The modern state...is an engine of propaganda, alternately manufacturing crises and pretending to be the only instrument that can deal effectively with them. This propaganda, to succeed, requires the cooperation of writers, teachers, and artists, not as paid propagandists or state-censored time-servers, but as 'free' intellectuals capable of policing their own jurisdictions and enforcing acceptable standards of accountability within the various intellectual professions." - Christopher Lasch "The Agony of the American Left," author of "Britain's Secret Propaganda War."

In Burnham's "The Managerial Revolution," he writes:

"Most of these intellectuals are completely unaware that the net social effect of the ideologies they elaborate contributes to the power and privilege of managers and the construction of a new structure of class dominance in society. As in the past, intellectuals believe that they speak for the truth and the interests of all mankind...In fact, the intellectual, without usually being aware of it, elaborates the new ideologies from the point of view of the position of the managers."

What this means is that the intellectuals themselves do not understand who it is that will ultimately benefit from the philosophies and theories they support and defend, they are mere instruments for the propagation of a new ruling class and hold no real power. Aldous

Huxley's speech, who also promoted a ruling class in his "Brave New World," to the naive students at Berkeley, entitled "The Ultimate Revolution," comes to mind....

As Huxley said:

"There will be, in the next generation or so, a pharmacological method of making people love their servitude, and producing a dictatorship without tears, as it were, producing a kind of painless concentration camp for whole societies, so that people will in fact have their liberties taken away, but rather enjoy it."

As noted above, Burnham had been recommended by George F. Kennan to head the semi-autonomous "Psychological Strategy Board" (PSB) division of the Office of Policy Coordination (OPC). PSB D-33/2, created on May 5, 1953, strategized on how "free intellectuals" could be manipulated against their own interests to facilitate a CIA-dictated transformation of Western culture. In fact, as Frances Stoner Saunder points out in "The Cultural Cold War," it was probably Burnham himself who drafted PSB D-33/2.

In "The Final Stage of the Machiavellian Elite Takeover of America," Paul Fitzgerald and Elizabeth Gould write:

"PSB D-33/2 predicts a 'long-term intellectual movement, to: break doctrinaire thought patterns worldwide' while 'creating confusion, doubt and loss of confidence' in order to 'objectively weaken the

intellectual appeal of neutralism and bias its adherents toward the spirit of the West.' The aim was to 'predispose local elites to the philosophy held by the planners,' while the employment of local elites would 'help to disguise the American origin of the effort to make it appear to be a native development.'"

Although declared as an antidote to Communist totalitarianism, an internal critic of the program, RSP officer Charles Burton Marshall, considered RSP D-33/2 itself to be appallingly totalitarian, interposing 'a broad doctrinal system' that 'accepts uniformity as a substitute for diversity,' embracing 'all fields of human thought - all fields of intellectual interests, from anthropology and artistic creations to sociology and scientific methodology.' He concluded: *"this is as totalitarian as it gets."*

With "The Machiavellians" Burnham had composed the handbook that forged the old Trotskyist left together with a right-wing Anglo-American elite. The political offspring of that volatile union would be called neoconservatism, whose overt mission would be to roll back Russian/Soviet influence everywhere. Its covert mission would be to reassert a British cultural dominance over the emerging Anglo/American Empire and maintain it through propaganda."

Burnham describes how it is necessary for the masses to believe that the revolution is beneficial to them, when in fact it is only the transition from one ruling class to another. The promise of some form of socialism free from the oppression of capitalism is offered, but the masses are told that real socialism will need time and can only be achieved later, in the meantime, a ruling class is put in place.

Burnham writes:

"Ideology must ostensibly speak in the name of 'humanity,' 'the people,' 'the race,' 'the future,' 'God,' 'destiny,' etc. Moreover, despite the opinion of many present-day cynics, not just any ideology is capable of appealing to the feelings of the masses. It is more than a problem of skillful propagandistic technique. A successful ideology has to appear to the masses, however confusedly, to actually express some of their own interests.

...At present, the ideologies that can have a powerful impact, that can really advance, are, naturally, the business ideologies, for they are the only ones that correspond to the real direction of events...In place of the 'individual,' the emphasis is on the 'state,' the people, the people, the race...In place of private enterprise, 'socialism' in name only or 'collectivism.' Instead of 'freedom' and 'free initiative', planning. Less talk of 'rights' and 'natural rights'; more of 'duties' and 'order' and 'discipline'. Less talk of 'opportunities' and more of 'jobs'."

He goes on to talk about the need to change the meaning of words like "destiny," "future," "sacrifice," "power," from the old ideologies of capitalism to fit the new ideologies of managerialism.

George Orwell would address this in his "1984," where Burnham's "The Managerial Revolution" appears under the pseudonym "Theory and Practice of Oligarchic Collectivism."

Burnham continues:

"There will not be a managerial ideology any more than there was a capitalist ideology. However, the various managerial ideologies will revolve around a common axis, just as the capitalist ideologies revolved around a common and different axis...In this country, technocracy and the much more important New-Dealism are embryonic and less developed types of primitive managerial ideologies, native to the United States."

Burnham's reference to New-Dealism as managerial politics may be troubling to some, however, Burnham only looks at the mechanics of a social situation and its potential uses in a managerial society, it does not mean that what he speaks of as it currently functions is a form of oppression upon the people. As Burnham states in his book, Roosevelt's New Dealism is not what was intended on paper, so to speak.

Burnham writes:

"The strongest representatives of the New Deal are not Roosevelt or the other conspicuous "New Deal politicians," but the younger group of administrators, experts, technicians, bureaucrats who have been finding their way into the whole state apparatus...in short, managers."

Keynes' vision for the New Deal was opposed to that of Roosevelt. Burnham expresses frustration that a man who had nothing to do with creating an idea is now pulling the strings, for more on this see here. An example of the type of New Deal Burnham refers to, suitable for his vision of a managerial society, can be found in the Green New Deal, or the anti-BRI Build Back Better for the World (aka: B3W).

These are the kind of ideologies that we are told will be universally beneficial, when in fact they are intended to benefit a select ruling class, in this case a managerial class, with the intention of maximizing global control to the detriment of the majority.

As Orwell said in his essay ***"Second Thoughts on Burnham"***:

"It will be seen that Burnham's theory is not, strictly speaking, a new theory. Many earlier writers have foreseen the emergence of a new kind of society, neither capitalist nor socialist, and probably based on slavery..."

The Great Reset: Oligarchic Collectivism.

"Wherein you radicals and we who hold opposite views differ is not so much the end as the means, not so much what is to be carried out, but how it should, and can, be carried out." - **Otto H. Kahn**

In his "Managerial Revolution," Burnham concludes:

"The new world political system based on a small number of superstates will still leave problems - more, perhaps, than a single unified world state; but it will be enough of a "solution" to keep society going. Nor is there any sufficient reason to believe that these managerial world system problems, including managerial wars, will "destroy civilization." It is almost inconceivable even what it could mean for civilization: to be literally destroyed. Once again: what is being destroyed is our civilization, not civilization."

For the destruction of our civilization, this is precisely the intention of the World Economic Forum and its affiliations with the Club of Rome/Henry Kissinger, and it is their intention that the very people who will be enslaved by such a ruling class, will ironically be the ones passionately fighting to see it ended. The masses themselves will be the ones willing to sacrifice and defend at all costs a growing power structure intended to bring about their own destruction.

61

Perhaps there are even those who know this and believe in such a cause, after all, if they agree that "the real enemy is humanity itself," as the Club of Rome concluded on the solution to humanity's problems, then the destruction of our civilization is not only justified, but it is our duty to carry it out.

But if that ideology turns out to be a sham, a fairy tale intended to benefit a select ruling class, its believers will be complicit in the commission of the most heinous crimes ever committed against humanity in our entire history of existence.

We are now at that precipice...

Orwell concludes in his "Second Reflection on Burnham":

"It is curious that in all his talk of the struggle for power, Burnham never pauses to ask why people want power. He seems to assume that the hunger for power, though it dominates only a comparatively small number of people, is a natural instinct that does not have to be explained, like the desire to eat. It also assumes that the division of society into classes serves the same purpose in all ages. This is practically ignoring the history of hundreds of years... The question that should be asked, and is never asked, is: Why does the lust for naked power become an important human motive precisely now, when man's dominion over man is ceasing to be necessary? As for the claim that "human nature," or the

"inexorable laws" of this and that, make socialism impossible, it is simply a projection of the past into the future. Indeed, Burnham argues that since a society of free and equal human beings has never existed, it can never exist. The same argument could have demonstrated the impossibility of airplanes in 1900, or automobiles in 1850.

...as long as they [the Nazis] were winning, Burnham seems to have seen nothing wrong with the methods of the Nazis...This implies that literally anything can become right or wrong if the ruling class of the moment wants it to...That a man of Burnham's gifts was able for a time to think of Nazism as something rather admirable, something that could and probably would build a viable and lasting social order shows, what damage is done to the sense of reality by the cultivation of what is now called 'realism'."

The Big Narrative 2021

With the upcoming launch of the "Grand Narrative" initiative in November, the World Economic Forum (WEF) intends to fix its officialist narrative of the Great Reset agenda in the collective mindset, to convince people why they need a Malthusian, technocratic, green Great Reset of society and the global economy. Once the Great Reset has its Grand Narrative, anything that goes against that narrative can be dismissed as conspiracy, disinformation or extremism that must be censored and suppressed "for the greater and collective good."

"The Grand Narrative initiative and the Dubai Gathering will be a powerful catalyst for shaping the contours of a more prosperous and inclusive future for humanity that is also more respectful of nature." - **Klaus Schwab, Director, World Economic Forum (2021)**

The Davos globalists, who never miss a good crisis, are once again exploiting the pandemic, this time to legitimize their agenda for a major reset of society and the global economy, calling for a "grand narrative" that can "help guide the creation of a more resilient, inclusive and sustainable vision for our collective future."

The WEF and its partners will contribute ideas for its narrative at the "Grand Narrative Meeting" in Dubai in November.

"The pandemic has highlighted the pressing need to focus on the long-term future and health of our societies," said WEF founder Klaus Schwab at the Davos Agenda.

"The Grand Narrative initiative and the Dubai meeting will be a powerful catalyst for shaping the contours of a more prosperous and inclusive future for humanity that is also more respectful of nature," he added.

"The Grand Narrative Initiative [is] a collaborative effort by the world's leading thinkers to shape long-term perspectives and co-create a narrative that can help guide the creation of a more resilient, inclusive and sustainable vision for our collective future."-**World Economic Forum, 2021**

According to the WEF, "The Grand Narrative Gathering is a centerpiece of the Grand Narrative initiative, a collaborative effort of the world's leading thinkers to shape long-term perspectives and co-create a narrative that can help guide the creation of a more resilient, inclusive and sustainable vision for our collective future."

Inclusivity, sustainability, resilience... these are terms Schwab himself used when he declared in June 2020, "Now is the time for a big reset."

At the grand narrative gathering in November, "leading thinkers from diverse geographies and disciplines- including futurists, scientists and philosophers-will contribute new ideas for the future. Their reflections will be shared in a forthcoming book, The Great Narrative, scheduled for publication in January 2022."

"The grand narrative has lost its credibility, regardless of the mode of unification it uses, regardless of whether it is a speculative narrative or an emancipatory narrative" - Jean-Francois Lyotard, "The Postmodern Condition: A Report on Knowledge" (1979).

The idea of a grand narrative is something French philosopher Jean-Francois Lyotard called a "grand narrative" (also known as a "metanarrative") that, according to Philo-Notes, "functions to legitimize power, authority, and social mores," i.e., everything the grand reset aims to achieve.

Authoritarians use grand narratives to legitimize their own power, and they do so by claiming to have knowledge and understanding that speak of a universal truth.

At the same time, authoritarians use these grand narratives in an "attempt to translate alternative narratives into their own language and to suppress all objections to what they themselves say."

Marxism creates "a society in which all individuals can develop their talents to the fullest" is an example of a grand narrative.

"Science has always been in conflict with narratives" - **Jean-Francois Lyotard**, "The Postmodern Condition: A Report on Knowledge" (1979).

"A good narrative trumps even the best data with solvency" - **Davos Agenda, 2015**

Historically, grand narratives such as Marxism ignore science, disdain alternative perspectives, and censor dissenting ideas.

In his 1979 book, "The Postmodern Condition: An Account of Knowledge," Lyotard argued, "The grand narrative has lost its credibility, regardless of the mode of unification it uses, regardless of whether it is a speculative narrative or a narrative of emancipation."

Lyotard believed that "science has always been in conflict with narratives" and that "judged by the yardstick of science, most of them turn out to be fables."

The WEF claims that its program of grand readjustment will help emancipate society from the unsustainable and unjust practices of shareholder capitalism.

But according to Lyotard's philosophy, the WEF's so-called grand narrative initiative lost its credibility the moment it was conceived.

And who are they recruiting to help craft their narrative?

Geneticists, futurists, philosophers, scientists and special interest groups who toe the line of the grand reset will be the ones to shape the grand narrative.

"In the battle for the hearts and minds of human beings, narrative will consistently outperform data in its ability to influence human thinking and motivate human action."- **Davos Agenda, 2015**

The World Economic Forum is well aware of the philosophy behind narratives and how to use them to manipulate human behavior.

According to a 2015 WEF blog post titled "How Narratives Influence Human Behavior," the World Bank guest author argues that "a good narrative trumps even the best data with creditability."

"In the battle for the hearts and minds of human beings, narrative will consistently outperform data in its ability to influence human thinking and motivate human action," he writes.

The author goes on to caution, "A false dichotomy has emerged between the use of narrative and data analysis; either can be equally misleading or useful in conveying the truth about causal effects."

It's a matter of trust.

Narratives are essential for telling stories and making sense of information.

According to Adventist Today, most religions behave like grand narratives in that they "purport to explain all of life, and other ways of looking at the world are interpreted as delusions or delusions."

Through its grand narrative initiative, will the WEF attempt to legitimize its grand top-down authoritarian revival by placing its ideology on a pedestal on the same moral level as the world's great religions?

"A false dichotomy has emerged between the use of narrative and data analysis; either can be equally misleading or useful in conveying the truth about causal effects."- Davos Agenda, 2015

The unelected globalists already have their slogan, "build back better," parroted by heads of state across the English-speaking world, from the United States to the United Kingdom, Australia, Canada and New Zealand.

Then comes the grand narrative, which the Davos elites will use in an attempt to legitimize their grand reset agenda.

Watch for even more coordinated messaging and information suppression by big tech, big government, business and corporate media on issues of:

- Climate change
- Carbon emissions
- Energy use
- New green agreements
- Alternative proteins
- Consumption
- Land use
- Cryptocurrencies
- Internet Governance
- Policy
- Disinformation
- Extremism
- Conspiracy theories

And many more.

"The pandemic has highlighted the imperative need to focus on the long-term future and health of our societies."- **Klaus Schwab, 2021**

Today, narratives are imposed through digital means, and anyone who disagrees can be displaced, demonetized, and even banned from participation in society, such as what is happening with the vaccine passports that are powering social credit and digital identity systems.

On his deathbed, Benjamin Franklin wrote his last essay, "Rules for Ruining a Republic," in which he wrote: "Words are to democracy as beams are to a house."

"Dissenting opinions should be called conspiracies, not judged by reason. Thus the beams are weakened and the house is easier to tear down."

Once the Great Reset has its Grand Narrative, anything that goes against that narrative can be dismissed as conspiracy, disinformation or extremism that must be censored and suppressed "for the greater and collective good."

Agenda 21

The Great Reset is a planned communist-style world government currently underway (by force) via the pre-planned and hoaxed Covid-19 pandemic. It is a totalitarian world program that became popular in 1987 through the United Nations. It was called Agenda 21, because the goal was to completely reset all governments and economies of the world by 2021. Since they are not able to finalize this goal by 2021 and had to extend their timeline (although they made massive progress this year, 2020, using this pandemic), Agenda 21 has been updated to Agenda 2030. This gives them ten more years to complete the global takeover.

Most Americans are blind to this invasion, because they trust corrupt politicians who are traitors to our laws and freedoms, and whose sole purpose is to set up a world communist government. And it is not just an unhappy future for America; all nations will be subject to the evil sway of this new, chimerical government. Its laws will devastate and dominate every aspect of our daily lives. By reading the list below, you can begin to see why this pandemic is a great tool for the globalists. Here are the drastic lifestyle changes we will experience in a few years if the citizens of our nation do not push back quickly.

In 1992, at the UN Earth Summit meeting, led by Secretary General Maurice Strong, Agenda 21 was established as a global force (a 1000 page report and booklet titled Agenda 21 was distributed with the details of the communist global agenda). It is important to mention that Maurice Strong was a dedicated supporter and resident of Communist China. Agenda 21/2030 is based on communism. And yet, Republican President George Bush, along with 177 other world leaders, embraced and supported this communist "New World Order", and signed on to Agenda 21. Bush's own 1991 speech confirmed his goal of putting America back under a New World Order.

Sustainable development

In order to convince the public to get on board with this communist "reset" of governments, Agenda 21/2030 is being peddled as part of a United Nations-founded "environmental safeguard" program called Sustainable Development. The partner organization, the International Institute for Sustainable Development (IISD), outlines and defines sustainable development as: "Development that meets the needs of the present without compromising the ability of future generations to meet their own needs. The simplest word to define sustainable development is communism.

To be even more precise, sustainable development is the code word for communism. Wherever you see an organization promoting sustainable development, or using the terms sustainable or sustainability (and almost every major corporation and university does), they are actually promoting the communist World Agenda 21/2030. Agenda 21 or Agenda 2030 is usually not mentioned as openly because the proponents prefer to hide their real goal for global communism under a "save the environment" theme. They know that people will not accept a communist lifestyle, but will commit themselves wholeheartedly to saving the planet. That is why, for example, the beliefs of "going green" and green gas and climate change have been forced upon the population and widely marketed.

The term sustainable development became popular after a 1987 UN report entitled, "Our Common Future," was released by the Brundtland Commission. The Commission is named after its chair, Gro Brundtland, former head of the World Health Organization (WHO) and the first female vice-president of the Socialist International. The globalists promoting Agenda 21 (now Agenda 2030) are using the term Sustainable Development to effectively infiltrate their communist agenda into American cities, counties and states; and other nations. This pandemic is now being used to implement the changes.

George Bush Sr. was not the only wolf who infiltrated the U.S. government with his communist views, deceiving his constituents. In 1993, President Clinton signed Executive Order 12852, which formed the "President's Council on Sustainable Development."

In 2011, President Obama went further to anchor Americans under Agenda 21. (Of course, unlike Bush and Clinton, Obama's campaign and presidency openly displayed his dedication to communism.) He signed Executive Order 13575, which established the "White House Rural Council." His order was devious. The first section reads:

"Sixteen percent of the American population lives in rural counties. Strong, sustainable rural communities are essential to winning the future and ensuring American competitiveness in the years ahead. These

communities provide our food, fiber, and energy, preserve our natural resources, and are essential to the development of science and innovation. While rural communities face many challenges, they also have tremendous economic potential. The federal government has an important role to play in expanding access to the capital needed for economic growth, promoting innovation, improving access to health care and education, and expanding outdoor recreation on public lands."

Sustainable Rural Communities in the first section indicates that Obama's newly formed "White House Rural Council" was designed to promote the United Nations' Agenda 21 plan. Obama's goal through this executive order was to fundamentally transform America.

Nearly every world leader, including President Biden, is behind the implementation of Agenda 21/2030 Sustainable Development as a new way of life, or in plain English, as a new tyrannical way of life under their new technocratic world order. The White House website reveals the truth that Biden agrees with liberal politicians past and present, and 100% behind the communist Sustainable Development agenda. On May 17, 2018, Biden signed Executive Order 13834, entitled "Effective Federal Operations." In this order, he has the authority to delegate a Chief Federal Sustainability Officer (please see "Implementing Instructions for Executive Order 13834 Efficient Federal Operations," from the Council on Environmental Quality, Federal Office of Sustainability), In 2021, Biden advanced the goals of the One World Agenda to 2030 by signing the U.S.-Mexico Agreement (USMCA).

He violated the legal roadmap of U.S. laws and signed this agreement without ratification by Congress or the Senate. Biden went further with the Agenda 2030 goals and on August 24, 2019, signed on with his "globalist" G7 allies (Canada, France, Germany, Italy, Japan, and the United Kingdom) to specifically direct sustainable development and other issues related to the globalization of nations.

The White House is 100% behind the Great Reset, and this 2015 pdf.doc, page 18, on the U.S. Agency for International Development (USAID) clearly states that world leaders have adopted the 2030 Agenda for Sustainable Development. Their vision of "open government to support global sustainable development" is set over a 15-year period (completion by 2030), the White House administration is committed to ensuring that efforts to implement the Sustainable Development Goals (SDGs) are open and transparent in consultation with civil society.

That's why the Agenda 21/2030 association called the International Council for Local Environmental Initiatives (ICLEI), shows more than 250 U.S. cities and counties that are members of this movement to restructure American government, economy and society. It also has more than 1,000 city leaders in 86 countries. But you can bet that membership now exceeds 250 U.S. cities. All of the West Coast state universities I googled are linked to the UN Sustainable Development Goals, as shown by Oregon State University, for example. I'm sure the Midwest and East Coast state universities have the same connections. All Covid-19 vaccine manufacturers, including AstraZeneca, promote sustainability on their websites. It's a global goal already in place around the world.

How can we trust the companies making Covid-19 vaccines when they support a global agenda that endorses depopulation? How can we be sure that their developed vaccines are truly safe for us and not to be used for sterility, long-term genocide, or DNA alteration for massive population mind control? Genetic modification is part of the technology on Covid-19 vaccines, so what will stop them from injecting us with vaccines that are genetically modified to cause cancer, genetic mutations, or chronic systemic diseases in order to advance their twisted mindset to mitigate the populations of nations? The websites of the various vaccine manufacturers indicate that they work closely with BARDA (Biomedical Advanced Research and Development Authority) and DARPA (Defense Advanced Research Projects Agency), two military agencies involved in biological weapons projects for the United States. The goals of forming a new government have been infiltrated at the highest levels worldwide, and therefore citizens of every country should question every politician, organization and vaccine company related to sustainable development.

World Economic Forum

Today, the main organization promoting Agenda 21/2030 for Sustainable Development is the World Economic Forum (WEF). The founder and chairman is billionaire professor Klaus Schwab. He is a communist ideologue and innovator who has been at the center of world affairs for over four decades. He is convinced that we are at the beginning of a revolution that will fundamentally change the way we live, work and connect with each other. And this pre-planned pandemic has effectively reignited his insane revolution, as he moves forward with his tyrannical plans to reshape the world under a new post-Covid 19 "twilight zone" utopia. The WEF website details what the post-Covid-19 world will look like by 2030, once the globalists achieve their goals.

The page on leadership and governance on the WEF website and their members and partners page is informative. But even more disturbing is that Schwab has recently published another book entitled: "COVID-19: The Great Reset." This book details what awaits America and the world after the planned pandemic achieves its goals of complete human control through Agenda 2030. The book states:

"COVID-19: The Great Reset is a guide for anyone who wants to understand how Covid-19 has disrupted our social and economic systems, and what changes will be

needed to create a more inclusive, resilient and sustainable world in the future."

Klaus Schwab is a force to be feared because his "Orwellian" cult has taken root around the world. World leaders, including President Trump, openly support Schwab's 2030 Agenda. News articles appear everywhere endorsing Schwab's Great Reset, as does Time Magazine. Biden himself was promoting WEF and Klaus Schwab on the White House website: whitehouse.gov.

Americans are naive to think that there is still a two-party system and that our votes count. This global agenda to control every aspect of our lives has been in motion for decades, and these infiltrated politicians have made giant strides in deceiving the public with hogwash promises. President Trump, for example, claims to be a conservative patriot, but he is far from loyal to this country. He follows the governance structure of Agenda 2030 and illegally allows local jurisdictions (county, city, state - like governors, mayors and health departments) to bypass the legislative process and create their own tyrannical and absurd executive orders (without medical science). The World Economic Forum, which is behind the 2030 Agenda, states on its website:

"Perhaps alternative centers of power - at the local or municipal level - can offer assurance and a faster way to get things done... All governments could do better by

*balancing autonomy and agility at the local level with
coordination at the national level."*

This statement is why President Biden relinquished his
authority over Covid-19's response and delegated his
power to state governors, who in turn relinquished
some of their authority to mayors and county
commissioners. Each of these governors and mayors,
etc., wrote their own different rules and regulations,
which created division and chaos (chaos weakens a
government). For example, some governors would
impose travel restrictions, curfews, or crazy restrictions
on firearms. Some would not allow citizens to visit their
own property if they owned a second home in the state,
buy paint, or allow travelers into their states without
14-day quarantine measures. The mayor of Los Angeles
made a rule that he would shut off electricity and water
to homes where large gatherings were taking place.
Where does this mayor get his authority for such
draconian measures? From President Trump. Biden has
participated in lockdowns, distancing and civil rights
violations by ignoring the supreme law of our land.
Instead, he followed the Agenda 2030 governance rules
that give more governance power to local jurisdictions.
It was a brilliant plan to dismantle our nation.

Further evidence of Trump's allegiance to the world
order is that he did nothing to stop the illegal orders of
any of these governors or mayors. Although we hear
him talk about inequity, we will never see him stop
injustice. That's because he is on board with the World

Economic Forum and Klaus Schwab and other world leaders in promoting a New World Order (which includes applying dangerous vaccinations to the population by military force).

The treachery is not just in our government. The U.S. military is the engine of this great reset of world communism. Communists have infiltrated America in every way possible. The military websites support the Sustainable Development Goals and that is why they have funded and partnered with all the Covid-19 vaccine manufacturers. Vaccines have nothing to do with our health, but everything to do with controlling our minds and bodies. They are part of the pre-planned hoax pandemic that is undermining our way of life in every way we can imagine. They will control what we eat, where we go, what we do and how we think if we do not rise together in unity and push back. They know that as they continue to deny Americans more freedoms, there will eventually be a huge opposition of armed Americans that will rise up. Instead of creating a bloody war in the streets and risking the loss of many of their own soldiers, it is much easier for them to disarm the people before a war can ensue by using a soft kill method, better known as a biological weapon. Vaccinating the population quickly (Operaton Warp Speed which uses the military to dispense vaccines to the population) is a brilliant tactic to eliminate hundreds of thousands of citizens without firing a single shot. Injecting them with toxic or DNA-altering vaccines would slowly paralyze the nation and allow the completion of the great New World Order reset.

Meanwhile, the constant illegal and unconstitutional ordinances are a gauge for the globalists. They are able to analyze the depths with which they can manipulate the masses. Once they are convinced that the people will not resist their tyranny, they will continue the takeover until their Agenda 2030 is fully implemented. One thing is certain, Agenda 2030 would not have been possible to accomplish this quickly and expeditiously without the Covid-19 pandemic. This pandemic was pre-planned to open the portal to the global elites' decades-long goal of ruling the world with an iron fist. There is a German federal pandemic response document (starting on page 55) published in 2012 that describes almost exactly a pandemic scenario as we see it today. The virus in their scenario is named "modi-sars" (modified coronavirus), which is far too close in similarities to the current Covid-19 virus. The paper is strange because it predicts that the pandemic will last 2-3 years, with "waves" of the virus returning, strict responses, food shortages, civil unrest and societal changes. This is a model for the current Covid-19 and global actions and responses. Event 201 (Event 201), a global pandemic exercise organized by the Johns Hopkins Center for Health Security, the World Economic Forum, and the Bill & Melinda Gates Foundation (all of whom support The Great Reset), suspiciously occurred on October 18, 2019, in New York City, just before the Covid-19 pandemic began. It is also important to note that the

Chinese CDC participated in this exercise. The 201 event pandemic scenario, like the German paper, also used a new simulated coronavirus and predicted that millions would die. It is no coincidence that the political, economic, religious and societal governances and pleasures of America and other countries are being rapidly destabilized by this pandemic, as was planned years ago.

Technocracy

The Agenda 2030 will be a new form of totalitarianism closely linked to technocracy. Technocracy is an ideological system of governance in which those in power (technocrats) control the masses and rule nations through advanced technical knowledge. This is one of the reasons why 5G wireless technology was important and deployed, despite the scientific evidence of its health hazards. The lockdowns, shutdowns and distancing are part of a conditioning to prepare the masses for this type of severely regulated lifestyle. In his book, "Between Two Ages: Americas Role in the Technetronic Era," former political guru and globalist Zbigniew Brzezinski argues that sovereignty is a fiction and that "the technetronic era implies a more controlled and directed society, dominated by an elite whose claim to political power would be based on allegedly superior scientific know-how using the latest modern techniques to influence public behavior and keep society under close surveillance and control."

Klaus Schwab's Great Reset is all about the age of technocracy. He wrote a book about this new age in 2016 called "The Fourth Industrial Revolution." Reviewers describe his book as follows: "Ubiquitous mobile supercomputing. Intelligent robots. Autonomous cars. Neuro-technological brain enhancements. Genetic editing. The evidence of dramatic change is all around us and it's happening at an exponential rate." Klaus, of course, wants technocracy to be used as a means to control the world's population for the benefit of those in power.

Here is a part from Schwab's WEF on globalization and what it means for the world and America coincides with his book on the Technocratic Age. Here is an excerpt: "The unprecedented pace of technological change means that our health, transportation, communication, production, distribution, and energy systems-to name a few-will be completely transformed. Managing this change will require not only new frameworks for national and multinational cooperation, but also a new model of education, with targeted programs to teach workers new skills. With advances in robotics and artificial intelligence in the context of aging societies, we will need to shift from a narrative of production and consumption to one of sharing and caring."

Bill Gates, the founder of Microsoft and the Bill and Melinda Gates Foundation, the eccentric billionaire who funded the push for depopulation and the new Covid-19 "RNA" vaccinations, also has his nose in the advancing age of technocracy. It has invested in new satellite technology, invested $85 million in the company Kymeta Satellite, and has a pending Microsoft patent called Cryptocurrency System Using Body Activity Data (WO/2020/060606). The patent is created to work in a digital cashless system by connecting people to a server where actual tasks are given and body energy and brain waves are generated and used to mine crypto currency. This, of course, is the goal of Agenda 2030: to control our finances through advanced technology. Once a government controls our bank accounts, it controls our lives. And this form of cashless buying and selling is not far off. Those who created this pandemic have caused lockouts and stand-down orders to condition the population to accept this new isolated banking structure. That's why House Democrats added language to the original $2 trillion CARES Act plan that called for the creation of a mandated U.S. digital dollar, through what they called the digital wallet. That didn't make it into the final bill, but eventually it will, as the new technocratic government moves forward with its global plans.

Billionaire entrepreneur Elon Musk, who is the force behind Tesla electric cars, is in tune with Klaus Schwab's disturbing technocratic ideology. Musk recently unveiled a wireless brain-computer implant for neuroscience that he calls Neuralink. Neuralink aims to implant wireless brain-computer interfaces comprising thousands of electrodes in the brain to help cure neurological conditions and spinal cord injuries. He has already had this coin-sized computer chip implanted in the brain of a pig for studies. This may sound plausible and like a great advance for medical science, but it's not. Musk's ultimate goal, like Bill Gates, is to merge humanity with artificial intelligence and create the perfect transhuman. Musk is on the same path as Gates and is also invested in satellites. Don't think for a minute that the global elite, the technocrats currently weighing their power over humanity, don't have the same goal in mind regarding the Covid-19 vaccine and their revolutionary new "gene editing."

Transhumanism

Technocracy cannot be accomplished until every person is inoculated. Their plans go beyond forcing the masses to stay home in front of their computers for the rest of their lives. They already have a much more nefarious and sinister agenda in place, and that is transhumanism, which is the control of the human body and the human mind by merging humanity with the machine. To do this, the globalists must modify our DNA with artificial DNA. Transhumanism is their ultimate goal to control the world because the globalists will have the capabilities to control the will of the people. They certainly won't tell us that they will alter our DNA and make us zombies because most people (I hope) would fight this theft of our minds.

The Covid-19 pandemic was the perfect tool to instill fear and panic, and get the population to accept mandatory vaccinations that contain artificial DNA that can irreversibly change our human genome forever. Does this sound absurd? Maybe 50 years ago, but in today's world, this technology is already developed. The goals for global control of nations are nothing new, and we should not be naïve in thinking that this form of slavery is not the ultimate "summit" for insane, power-hungry leaders.

In May 2010, the Rockefeller Foundation, in conjunction with futurist Peter Schwartz's Global Business Network, released a prophetic report (more evidence that the

Covid-19 pandemic was pre-planned) entitled: "Scenarios for the Future of Technology and International Development." This report contains various future-type scenarios. One scenario appears to be an accurate model for current Covid pandemic responses and actions. It has the intriguing subtitle: "LOCK STEP: A world of tighter government control and more authoritarian leadership, with limited innovation and increasing citizen revulsion." This section states:

"In 2012, the pandemic the world had been predicting for years finally struck. Unlike the 2009 H1N1 flu, this new strain of flu - from wild geese - was extremely virulent and deadly. Even the most pandemic-prepared countries were quickly overwhelmed as the virus swept across the globe, infecting nearly 20% of the world's population and killing 8 million people in just seven months... The pandemic also had a deadly effect on economies: the international mobility of people and goods came to a halt, weakening industries such as tourism and breaking global supply chains. Even locally, normally bustling stores and office buildings sat empty for months, without employees or customers."

The excerpt continues and is quite chilling: "During the pandemic, national leaders around the world flexed their authority and imposed airtight rules and restrictions, from mandatory face masks to body temperature checks at entrances to common spaces like train stations and supermarkets. Even after the pandemic had passed, this more authoritarian control and surveillance of citizens and their activities remained stable and even intensified. In order to protect against the spread of increasingly global problems - from pandemics and transnational terrorism to environmental crises and growing poverty - people everywhere have taken a firmer grip on power."

There is no doubt that this pandemic was a pre-planned tool to implement a new world order and reset the lives of every human being. This reset of nations and America is underway and it is too late to vote. Each new president will implement what is already in place under the Sustainable Development Goals. The roots of Agenda 21 began under the UN, by communists in China. And now the U.S. government and military are on their knees in partnerships with China to develop the wrong Covid-19 vaccines. This is treason against American values and freedoms. Pfizer Covid-19 vaccine company is partnered with Fosun, the Chinese vaccine company in Shanghai, and like Pfizer, Fosun is in bed with the Sustainable Development Goals. Pfizer is also partnered with the Chinese pharmaceutical company CanSinoBIO. A simple Google search will show how many Chinese have been and are currently linked to American and European companies. It is no mere coincidence that this pandemic started in China, or that our leaders are following China's draconian responses to the pandemic and taking away our rights. China is already part of our government. And don't think Russia is perfectly clean. They are one with China and this global reset, and just as thrilled to have their vision of communism outshine the free world.

Biden, an avowed communist, will soon be the new president, which means deeper problems for America. We have a chance to push back and thwart the global plans by resisting and refusing to take the Covid-19 vaccine. They need all of us vaccinated to accomplish and finalize this new extreme dictatorial technocratic government. They cannot gain total control of the masses until they inject these genetically modified vaccines into our bodies and modify our human genome with their synthetic materials. Once vaccinated, we become transhuman and putty in their hands for total control of our moods, behaviors and thoughts. Stealing our minds through deception is exactly their plan of action. Therefore, let's beat this New World Order and resist the tyranny, and part of stopping the Great Reset is stopping the vaccine!

Zero carbon corporatism

The globalist World Economic Forum in Davos proclaims the need to achieve a global goal of "net zero carbon" by 2050. This seems for the most part far into the future and therefore largely ignored. Yet the transformations underway from Germany to the United States to countless other economies are setting the stage for the creation of what was called in the 1970s the New International Economic Order. In reality, it is a blueprint for a global technocratic totalitarian corporatism, which promises enormous unemployment, deindustrialization and economic collapse by design. Consider some background. Klaus Schwab's World Economic Forum (WEF) is currently promoting its pet theme, the great reset of the global economy. The key to all this is to understand what the globalists mean by Net Zero Carbon by 2050. The EU is leading the race, with a bold plan to become the world's first "carbon neutral" continent by 2050 and reduce its CO_2 emissions by at least 55% by 2030.

In an August 2020 blog post, self-proclaimed global vaccine czar Bill Gates wrote of the coming climate crisis, "As horrible as this pandemic is, climate change could be worse... The relatively small drop in emissions this year makes one thing clear: we can't get to zero emissions simply - or even primarily - by flying and driving less."

With a near-monopoly on mainstream media as well as social media, the global warming lobby has been able to get much of the world to assume that the best thing for humanity is to eliminate hydrocarbons, including oil, natural gas, coal, and even "carbon-free" nuclear power by 2050, to give us hope that we can avoid a 1.5 to 2 degree centigrade increase in global average temperature. There is only one problem with this. It's a cover for an unspoken criminal agenda.

Origins of "global warming

Many have forgotten the original scientific thesis put forward to justify a radical change in our energy sources. It was not "climate change". The Earth's climate is constantly changing, correlated with changes in solar flare emissions or sunspot cycles affecting the Earth's climate. At the turn of the millennium, when the previous solar warming cycle was no longer evident, Al Gore and others shifted the narrative in a linguistic sleight of hand from "Global Warming" to "Climate Change". Now the scare narrative has become so absurd that every abnormal weather event is treated as a "climate crisis." Every hurricane or winter storm is claimed as evidence that the climate gods are punishing us sinful CO_2-emitting humans.

But wait. The whole reason for the transition to alternative energy sources such as solar or wind power, and the abandonment of carbon-based energy sources, is their claim that CO_2 is a greenhouse gas that somehow rises into the atmosphere where it forms a blanket that is supposed to warm the Earth below. - Global warming. According to the U.S. Environmental Protection Agency, most greenhouse gas emissions come from CO2. Hence the emphasis on "carbon footprints".

What is almost never said is that CO2 cannot rise into the atmosphere from car exhaust, coal-fired power plants or other man-made sources. Carbon dioxide is not carbon or soot. It is an invisible, odorless gas that is essential for photosynthesis in plants and all life on earth, including us. CO2 has a molecular weight of just over 44 while air (mainly oxygen and nitrogen) has a molecular weight of only 29. The density of CO2 is about 1.5 times that of air. This would suggest that CO2 exhaust from vehicles or power plants does not rise into the atmosphere about 12 miles or more above the Earth to form the feared greenhouse effect.

To appreciate what criminal action is taking place today around Gates, Schwab and the proponents of a supposedly "sustainable" global economy, one must go back to 1968 when David Rockefeller and his friends created a movement around the idea that human consumption and population growth were the world's main problem. Rockefeller, whose wealth was based on oil, created the Neo-Malthusian Club of Rome in the Rockefeller Villa in Bellagio, Italy. Their first project was to fund an unwanted study at MIT called The Limits to Growth in 1972.

One of the main organizers of Rockefeller's "zero growth" program in the early 1970s was his longtime friend, a Canadian oilman named Maurice Strong, also a member of the Club of Rome. In 1971, Strong was appointed under-secretary of the United Nations and secretary-general of the Earth Day conference in Stockholm in June 1972. He was also a trustee of the Rockefeller Foundation. (Read: "The Fabian Society: The Masters of Subversion Unmasked")

Maurice Strong was an early key propagator of the scientifically unfounded theory that man-made emissions from transportation vehicles, coal-fired power plants, and agriculture have caused a dramatic and accelerating increase in global temperature that threatens civilization, so-called global warming. He coined the elastic term "sustainable development".

As chairman of the United Nations Stockholm Earth Day Conference in 1972, Strong encouraged population reduction and lowering of world living standards to "save the environment." A few years later, the same Strong declared:

"Isn't the only hope for the planet that industrialized civilizations will collapse? Isn't it our responsibility to make this happen?

This is the agenda known today as the Great Reset or the United Nations 2030 Agenda. Strong went on to

97

create the Intergovernmental Panel on Climate Change (IPCC), a political body that advances the unproven claim that man-made CO_2 emissions were about to tip our world into irreversible ecological catastrophe.

The co-founder of the Club of Rome, Dr. Alexander King, admitted the essential fraud of their environmental agenda some years later in his book, The First Global Revolution. He stated, "In looking for a new enemy to unite us, we got the idea that pollution, the threat of global warming, water shortages, famine, etc. would do the trick... All of these dangers are caused by human intervention and only through changed attitudes and behavior can they be overcome. The real enemy, therefore, is humanity itself."

King admitted that the "threat of global warming" was just a ploy to justify an attack on "humanity itself." It is now being deployed as the great reset and ruse of "Net Zero Carbon".

Alternative energy disaster

In 2011, on the advice of Joachim Schnellnhuber of the Potsdam Institute for Climate Impact Research (PIK), Angela Merkel and the German government imposed a total ban on nuclear power by 2022, as part of a 2001 government strategy called the Energiewende or Energy Turn, to rely on solar and wind power and other "renewables." The goal was to make Germany the first industrial nation to be "carbon neutral."

The strategy has been an economic disaster. From having one of the most stable and reliable power systems in the industrial world, Germany has now become the most expensive power generator in the world. According to the German energy industry association BDEW, by 2023 at the latest, when the last nuclear power plant closes, Germany will be facing electricity shortages. At the same time, coal, the largest source of electrical energy, is being phased out to achieve "Net Zero Carbon". Traditional energy-intensive industries such as steel, glass production, basic chemicals, paper and cement manufacturing, are facing soaring costs and closures or relocation and the loss of millions of skilled jobs. Energy-efficient wind and solar power now cost some 7 to 9 times more than gas.

Germany has little sunshine compared to tropical countries, so wind is considered the main source of green energy. There is a huge input of concrete and aluminum needed to produce solar or wind farms. This requires cheap energy - gas, coal or nuclear - to produce. As this is eliminated, the cost becomes prohibitive, even without a "carbon tax" added.

Germany already has some 30,000 wind turbines, more than anywhere else in the European Union. Gigantic wind turbines have serious noise or infrasound problems for the health of residents near the huge structures and damage from weather and birds. By 2025, an estimated 25% of existing German wind turbines will need to be replaced and waste disposal is a huge problem. Companies are being sued as citizens realize how catastrophic they are. To meet targets by 2030, Deutsche Bank recently admitted that the state will have to create an "ecological dictatorship.

At the same time, Germany's push to end gasoline or diesel transportation by 2035 in favor of electric vehicles is poised to destroy Germany's largest and most profitable industry, the automotive sector, and eliminate millions of jobs.

Lithium-ion battery-powered vehicles have a total "carbon footprint" when the effects of lithium extraction and production of all parts are included, which is worse than diesel cars. And the amount of additional electricity needed for a zero-carbon Germany by 2050 would be far greater than it is today, because millions of battery chargers will need grid electricity with reliable power.

Now Germany and the EU are starting to impose new "carbon taxes," ostensibly to fund the transition to zero carbon. The taxes will only make electricity and energy even more expensive, ensuring a faster collapse of German industry.

Depopulation

According to those who advance the Zero Carbon agenda, this is exactly what they want: the deindustrialization of the most advanced economies, a strategy calculated over several decades as Maurice Strong has said, to bring about the collapse of industrialized civilizations.

Rolling back the current global industrial economy to a dystopia of wood heat and windmills where blackouts become the norm as they are today in California, is an essential part of a grand reset transformation under the Agenda 2030: UN Global Compact for Sustainability.

Merkel's climate advisor, Joachim Schnellnhuber, an atheist, presented Pope Francis' radical green agenda, the encyclical letter Laudato si', in 2015 as a member of the Pontifical Academy of Sciences. And he advised the EU on its green agenda. In a 2015 interview, Schnellnhuber said that "science" has now determined that the maximum carrying capacity of a "sustainable" human population is about six billion people less: "In a very cynical way, this is a triumph for science because we have finally stabilized something - namely the estimates of the carrying capacity of the planet, namely less than one billion people."

To do this, the industrialized world must be dismantled. Christiana Figueres, an agenda contributor to the World Economic Forum and former executive secretary of the United Nations Framework Convention on Climate Change, revealed the true purpose of the UN climate agenda at a press conference in Brussels in February 2015, where she said, "This is the first time in history that we have set ourselves the task of intentionally changing the model of economic development that has prevailed since the industrial revolution."

Figueres' words in 2015 are echoed today by French President Macron at the January 2021 World Economic Forum's "Davos Agenda," where he said that "under the current circumstances, the capitalist model and the open economy are no longer feasible." Macron, a former Rothschild banker, argued that "the only way out of this epidemic is to create an economy that is more focused on eliminating the gap between rich and poor." Merkel, Macron, Gates, Schwab and their friends will do this by bringing the standard of living in Germany and the OECD down to that of Ethiopia or Sudan. This is their zero-carbon dystopia.

Severely limiting air travel, car travel, people travel, closing down "polluting" industries, all to reduce CO_2 emissions. It is amazing how the coronavirus pandemic paves the way for the Great Reset and the United Nations 2030 Agenda "Net Zero Carbon".

Our future

On May 24, the organization "Stop World Control" produced a film entitled "The Battle For Humanity" in which Dr. Carrie Madej makes a strong case that the Covid-19 "vaccine" injections are altering human DNA and facilitating transhumanism.

The Stop World Control organization was founded by David Sorensen, author, speaker, designer, artist and coach. Stop World Control is a platform for the voices of many freedom warriors who will not be led to slaughter. It is the result of sincere research and honest observation, while wisely trying not to fall into the trap of unfounded conspiracy theories.

In the film "The Battle For Humanity" it is said: "The active ingredient in the Moderna vaccine that alters our RNA or DNA is called "luciferase".

Is this code for "Lucifer / Erase" humanity (Lucifer / Erase)?"

Dr. Carrie Madej warns in the film that COVID injections have two purposes:

1. Reprogram our DNA to make us easier to control human-IA hybrids.

2. Implant a Digital Vaccine ID that will allow total control over each person.

The Stop World Control website warns, "There is a battle raging for humanity.

Dr. Carrie Madej reveals how Big Tech is collaborating with Big Pharma to introduce new technologies in future vaccines that will alter our DNA and turn us into hybrids. This will end humanity as we know it and start the process of transhumanism: HUMAN 2.0

The plans are to use vaccines to inject nanotechnology into our bodies and connect us to the Cloud and artificial intelligence. This will allow corrupt governments and tech giants to control us, without us being aware of it."

While a growing number of scientists and doctors have warned of the dangers of COVID injections (as outlined below), Dr. Madej is unique in explaining that the true purpose of the injections is to transform human beings (Human 1.0) into fused transhumans with Artificial Intelligence (Human 2.0) without our knowledge or consent. This technology will be used to control each person to levels never before possible.

Dr. Madej explains that we are currently living in the most pivotal time in human history.

She shows that this is World War III, a spiritual war of the mind, heart and soul. She explains how we can win now.

Dr. Madej says he learned at scientific and business meetings that there is another program to include hydrogel (nanotechnology) in COVID "vaccines." The hydrogel can send and receive data wirelessly via your phone. It goes through 5G to a super computer that analyzes it and can give you a crypto-currency based on your actions.

Dr. Madej reports that on March 26, 2020, Microsoft patent 060606 was published. She says Microsoft patented a crypto-currency mining system that harnesses human activities, including brain waves and body heat when performing online tasks such as using search engines, chat bots and reading ads. This technology allows the people controlling it to know each other's thoughts, emotions, location, whether they are drinking alcohol, having sex, ovulating, etc. In business meetings that Dr. Madej attended, it was announced that this technology would soon be implemented without telling the public.

This is a complete loss of autonomy and privacy with plans to use the technology as "predictive policing" like in The Minority Report. In July 2020, Bill Gates introduced digital identification in West Africa based on vaccination history. People there who have received COVID vaccines have hydrogel (nanobots) in them. Gates is proud that this is related to predictive policing. Dr. Madej explains that once this technology is perfected in West Africa, it will go to all developed countries. Bill Gates talks about controlling human behavior around the world. This is the real reason he insisted that the world receive the precipitous injections of COVID - to protect no one from a "deadly pandemic."

Dr. Madej raises key questions about the COVID "vaccines" in his interview for the documentary Planet Lockdown. Only by hiding this information have millions of Americans volunteered to participate in this unprecedented, dangerous and unnecessary experiment. They are being injected without the informed consent required by the Nuremberg Code. Unfortunately, some schools and employers are forcing these injections.

Catherine Austin Fitts shows that the reason COVID injections are called "vaccines" is to allow them an exemption from liability. In addition, calling them vaccines allows them to be issued under the emergency use authorization that can only be used for vaccines. Even if these injections were vaccines, the EUAs for these injections are still illegal since there are at least four COVID treatments.

Dr. Madej shows that the shots inject nanotechnology to collect data and create patented people. Who owns them? She says the technology injects biosensors that will be the basis for the crypto-currencies people will get. The "inoculated" people will be connected to the Internet of Everything where their biometric data will be transmitted to supercomputers. This is how the authorities get implants in people - without their knowledge or consent. Many people would have resisted an implant as - Mark of the Beast - especially one that determines how they can buy and sell - because the Bible warns against it. So, by calling this technology a "vaccine," the authorities are encouraging people to get chipped. Dr. Madej mentions Bill Gates' ID 2020, which is a plan for every person to have an ID.

Thus, the "health" policies of COVID-19 have been a multi-faceted Trojan horse that people have welcomed to save them from a "deadly pandemic," but which not only paralyzes and kills people on a massive scale, but also enslaves them. in multiple ways. It is a campaign based on a multi-faceted deception. Dr. Madej says these policies are not based on sound science and clearly indicate that there is a global agenda that involves the surveillance and control of every human being. She says this is the ultimate in slavery because technology allows for the control of bodies and minds.

Dr. Madej says this is the most crucial point in human history. She says, "If we don't have our freedom, what do we have?" She says we are in a great war - the war between good and evil and a great awakening is now taking place. "We are awakening now to what has been going on in the world for a long time: deception and lies, oppression and slavery at different levels. The line has been drawn. Which side are you on? What else is there but freedom and love?"

Dr. Madej encourages people to check out the Heart Math Institute, which has found that heart energy comes out six feet. So that's probably why social distancing forces people to stay 6 feet apart - to prevent heart-to-heart connection, just as masks undermine emotional connections.

Dr. Madej says, "We can make it better. We need to remember who we are. Once we do, we will see bright, happy people, the Light coming from everyone. What a wonderful world - but first we have to get through the ugliness to see what we have been hypnotized, brainwashed, oppressed by. It's hard, we all know that, but the good thing is that there is a good ending. We get to come back to our true natural selves which is a beautiful and brilliant Being of Light. It's just that little fire that we have to light in everyone so that they remember."

Shady business in Europe?

While some Europeans continue to resist compulsory vaccination measures, a group of parliamentarians has censured the Commission for allowing pharmaceutical companies to "trample on democracy".
One of the most important lessons you learn in life is that you should never buy a product before reading all the fine print in the contract. Caveat emptor," as all subjects of the Roman Empire instinctively understood.

However, it seems that few Brussels bureaucrats have lately bought a new house, a used car or some novelty device, because that is exactly what these bumbling fools have done. In an effort to "protect the health of their constituents," they bought millions of lots of Covid vaccines from various pharmaceutical companies without letting lawmakers take a look at the contracts.

It turns out that entire pages of these documents - the few that have been made public - have been heavily redacted. This has raised more than one eyebrow in the European Union, and perhaps none more striking than that of Romanian MEP Cristian Terhes.

Over the weekend, Terhes appeared at a press conference in Brussels with several other EU lawmakers from this side, all of them visibly shocked by the news that they would be required to present, as of November 3, a digital "green pass" in order to enter Parliament. Like many EU citizens, these legislators have refused the vaccine not because they are "anti-vaccine," but because they have been denied critical information about the product and procedures. Now they will be denied entry to Parliament, the place where the will of their people is (supposedly) represented.

Terhes revealed that, back in January, EU lawmakers were demanding "full access to the contracts signed between these companies producing the vaccines and the European Union." To say that the parliamentarians were disappointed would be an understatement.

The Romanian MEP, who represents the Christian Democrat National Peasant Party, cited an article in Euractiv that reported, "The contract, signed between the pharmaceutical company CureVac and the European Commission in November, was made available to MEPs [on January 12, 2021] in a redacted format after the company agreed to open the contract to scrutiny."

This is really putting the cart before the horse, because how can something that has been so crudely redacted be opened up to scrutiny? Terhes denounced that Brussels is "imposing a medical product on European citizens without them knowing what is in these contracts." That is simply inexcusable and should be easily struck out even by a third-rate lawyer.

More surprising is that even EU MEPs do not know the details of the agreements.

To prove his point, the Romanian MEP showed individual pages of the CureVac contract, each heavily redacted as a sort of imitation of artist Kazimir Malevich's "Black Square." The matter does not cease to be worrying when one analyzes which parts of the contract were crossed out. According to an analysis by Euractiv, "4.22% of the liability section and 15.38% of the indemnity section were redacted, while 0% of the section on the processing of personal data was redacted."

On the other hand, the annexes to the contract, which delve into the details of the agreement, were 61% redacted. In total, almost 24% of the contract was concealed. Now ask yourself this simple question: would you sign a mortgage if it was discovered that a quarter of the agreement was missing? I'll go out on a limb and say no. Nor would anyone think you were 'anti-mortgage' or 'mortgage undecided' if you did.

The truth is that you, and millions of other rational people exactly like you, are simply 'pro-transparency'. Yet these medical consumers are treated as second-class citizens for simply wanting more information before agreeing to be injected with something. 'My body, my choice' is a rallying cry that no longer applies, as millions are fast discovering, in today's authoritarian climate.

It should be noted that it is on the basis of these contracts that Europeans must come to a decision, based on "informed consent", that they will 'voluntarily' take the injection in order not to be ostracized from polite society. Unless they agree to take one of the available vaccines, EU citizens face the prospect of being denied the right to work, enter a store, buy medicine, take their children to school and travel freely from one country to another.

Naturally, this makes the stakes for not taking the vaccine incredibly high, but that only makes it worse that the details are deliberately hidden from the public. It's no secret that the pharmaceutical giants enjoy full compensation in the event that a person suffers a death or injury after receiving a Covid injection. And while such unfortunate occurrences appear to be rare, even Pfizer-BioNTech, which has received approval to extend vaccination to children aged 12 to 15 in the EU, seems unsure what the long-term effects of the vaccines may be.

"Other adverse reactions, some of which may be serious, may become apparent with more widespread use of Pfizer-BioNTech's Covid-19 vaccine," it states clearly on its website.

In February, the Bureau of Investigative Journalism published a damning report on Pfizer, claiming that the pharmaceutical company's negotiators had behaved in a "bullying" manner with several Latin American countries. In Argentina they demanded "additional compensation" against civilians seeking legal redress after suffering adverse effects from their vaccines. In the agreements, Pfizer ensures that all financial responsibility for compensating citizens harmed by the inoculations rests with the respective government.

The company also enjoys the protection of non-disclosure agreements with many of its domestic customers, including the European Commission and the U.S. government. With respect to the EU, Brussels is prohibited from disclosing information that would be "material to Pfizer without Pfizer's consent," Public Citizen reported.

In fact, CureVac was being quite generous with the EU Commission, considering it was the only pharmaceutical company agreeing to make its contract public. Of course, there wasn't much to inspect with all the redactions, but beggars can't be choosers, right?

In light of the constant pressure on Brussels, much of it behind closed doors, the European Commission has obliquely admitted - almost a year late, and after the rights and freedoms of European citizens have been crushed - that it did not use good judgment in approving these emergency vaccines.

Last week, in a resolution passed overwhelmingly (458 in favor, 149 against and 86 abstentions), the EU Parliament demanded legislation that would make "the process of researching, purchasing and distributing Covid-19 vaccines more transparent, stating:

"This would allow MEPs to effectively scrutinize EU vaccine policies. At the same time, the Commission should discuss these policies more openly with citizens."

This shocking statement from the EU Parliament demonstrates how little respect Brussels had for democratic principles when negotiating with vaccine manufacturers, who, by the way, have reaped a windfall from the pandemic. The parliamentarians, who are being criticized at home, demanded that "the Commission reveal who negotiates vaccine purchases on its behalf. It should publish the purchase agreements concluded with vaccine suppliers, including details of public investments and vaccine costs, and make public any possible breaches of contract."

Next, in what amounts to the understatement of the century, MEPs opine that "more information could help counter doubts and misinformation about vaccines, and pharmaceutical companies should also publish extensive data and clinical trial reports."

Oh yeah?

The next question is not idle: why are MEPs ONLY NOW talking about the total lack of transparency and democracy that occurred between the EU Commission and Big Pharma? A more cynical person would be tempted to say that it is because the draconian vaccine mandates have finally reached the very door of the Parliament, where the power brokers are locked in their offices, as are thousands of people in the street. Welcome to the club.

In any case, the fact that Brussels has concealed the details of its agreements with vaccine manufacturers for almost a year, while casually destroying the civil liberties of its citizens, totally disqualifies them from punishing those who are "undecided" about receiving the vaccine. "Informed consent" is essential to any functioning democracy, and Europeans were clearly denied that right. Do the right thing, Brussels, and release these heavy chains from your people. The world is watching.